Social Meanings of Religious Experiences

SERIES IN AMERICAN STUDIES

Editor-in-Chief: Joseph J. Kwiat

PROGRAM IN AMERICAN STUDIES
UNIVERSITY OF MINNESOTA

SOCIAL MEANINGS

OF

RELIGIOUS EXPERIENCES

BY

GEORGE DAVIS HERRON

With a New Introduction by
TIMOTHY L. SMITH
PROFESSOR OF EDUCATION AND OF HISTORY
THE JOHNS HOPKINS UNIVERSITY

JOHNSON REPRINT CORPORATION

New York and London

1969

The edition reproduced here was originally
published in 1896.

Library of Congress Catalog Card Number: 74-79658

Printed in the U. S. A.

INTRODUCTION

At a critical moment in the awakening of the Christian conscience to urban social problems in America, George D. Herron, Professor of Applied Christianity at what is now Grinnell College, appeared on university campuses across the nation to set forth a spiritual and Biblical plea for Christian socialism. This book, one of a half dozen that he published between 1891 and 1896, exhibits the persuasive way in which Herron associated a radically new social philosophy with the traditional ideas of Protestant evangelicals. He interpreted both Biblical and modern forms of religious experience in such a manner as to make them a foundation for social reconstruction.

American Protestants had from earliest colonial times been preoccupied with the problem of individual conversion. Their uprooting and migration from Europe and their frequent resettlement in the New World set individuals adrift from both the institutions and the rituals which had once surrounded their lives, giving free play to the mystical and evangelical strain in Christian piety. The establishment of voluntary congregations in the first colonies and, later, the fashioning of denominational organizations to sustain them, helped to prevent the disorder which religious individualism threatened to produce. The result, plainly evident by the middle of the eighteenth century, was to focus the attention of American ecclesiastical leaders inward, upon their own followers and upon the new structures of church order which they believed would maintain stability and traditional morality on the ever-expanding frontier. Thereafter, the experiment in the separation of church and state, first practiced in Pennsylvania and New York, then enshrined in the Federal Constitution, confirmed both the evangelical definition of religion's social role and the system of denominationalism which was its logical corollary.

During the first decades of the nineteenth century revivalists managed to recover a wider view of the social and national purposes of individual conversion. They set out, then, to lead the religious denominations in a cooperative effort to build a Kingdom of God in

America. The missions to the Mississippi Valley, the benevolent and educational activities directed toward the urban poor, and the crusade to free enslaved Negroes nurtured a movement toward Christian reform which Methodists, Presbyterians, Baptists and Congregationalists shared quite as fully as Quakers and Unitarians. Their method was persuasion, not coercion; their aim was a pluralistic but Protestant society in which God's "higher law" would reign supreme.

This mid-nineteenth-century social awakening, rooted in Biblical and spiritual faith, continued without significant interruption through the decades of Civil War and Reconstruction. True, preachers of conservative bent opposed "politics in the pulpit" and, especially in the post-war South, placed heavy emphasis on the merely pietistic aspects of conversion. By the 1880's, however, progressive evangelicalism was firmly rooted in the Protestant consciousness of all sections. Lyman Abbott and Washington Gladden, to name two Congregationalists, as well as Frederic Dan Huntington and Frances Wil-

lard, to name an Episcopalian and a Methodist, were by then promoting Christian social
reforms which seemed to contemporaries as
American as apple pie.

Meanwhile, however, the issue of economic
justice had assumed critical importance. The
underlying causes of this development were
the swift expansion of the industrial revolution, the accelerating growth of large cities,
the ignorance and poverty of the former slave
population, and the influx of unprecedented
millions of immigrants, many of whom were
Roman Catholic and Eastern Orthodox
Christians from Southern and Central Europe, or Orthodox Jews from Russia, Poland
and the Austro-Hungarian Empire. Open
warfare between organized labor and the
owners of railroads, mines, and factories, as
well as the deepening tragedy of share-crop
farming and Jim Crow laws in the South,
dramatized this economic issue. Inevitably,
the dialogue between Marxism and capitalism
spilled over from Europe into the United
States.

George D. Herron, who became after 1894

the leader of the most radical wing of the movement toward social Christianity, determined that the churches must squarely face the problem of economic injustice. Ordained to the Congregational ministry in 1884, but with little theological training, Herron served a succession of small-town pastorates in the Upper Midwest until 1890, when his address before the Minnesota Congregational Club, entitled "The Message of Jesus to Men of Wealth," aroused widespread comment. Soon after, he became associate pastor of the First Congregational Church at Burlington, Iowa, where he developed his social views in volumes of lectures and sermons bearing such titles as *The Larger Christ; A Plea for the Gospel; The Call of the Cross;* and *The New Redemption: A Call to the Church to Reconstruct Society According to the Gospel of Christ.*

In 1893, a wealthy woman who was a member of the Burlington congregation endowed a chair of Applied Christianity for Herron at Iowa College, soon to be renamed Grinnell. He began teaching there in the fall of that year, exciting almost immediately such widespread interest among laymen and pastors in the surrounding towns that his lectures had to be moved to the college chapel to accommodate the crowds. The endowment also financed the appearance of numerous guest lecturers on the Grinnell campus. Among these were Graham Taylor, Professor of Christian Sociology at the Chicago Theological Seminary; Hamlin Garland, who gave literary expression to agricultural discontent on the Midwestern frontier; evangelist Benjamin Fay Mills, a leading Presbyterian advocate of social Christianity; and Charles M. Sheldon, Congregationalist pastor at Topeka, Kansas, who was soon to publish the famous tract of the social awakening entitled *In His Steps, Or What Would Jesus Do*. Early in 1894 Herron embarked on the first of his long preaching tours to colleges and seminaries across the country. The result was a fifth book, *The Christian Society*.

The young professor was meanwhile active as secretary of the American Institute of Christian Sociology, founded at Chautauqua,

New York, in 1893. Its leaders included Richard T. Ely, Professor of Economics at the University of Wisconsin, Washington Gladden, Congregationalist pastor at Columbus, Ohio, and Methodist Bishop John H. Vincent. Herron served as the "organizer" and "principal of instruction" for the Institute, and became its third president in 1895. That same year Walter Rauschenbusch and others began the publication in New York of a periodical entitled *The Kingdom* which served as the organ of the association.

Within two years of his appointment at Grinnell, however, Herron's increasing social and theological radicalism and his sharp attacks on the conservatism of denominational leaders subjected him to a mounting tide of criticism. His health failed, and he took a leave of absence from the college to travel and study abroad. What he had called the "Kingdom Movement" never recovered its vitality.

Many who had shared in it, however, continued to promote the growth of social Christianity in America. In 1903, Edward

E. Carr, a Methodist who had withdrawn
from his denomination to become pastor of a
"people's" church, joined the Socialist Party
and began publishing a journal entitled *The
Christian Socialist*. Three years later, Carr
helped organize the Christian Socialist Fellowship. As time passed, several organizations and journals joined in a widespread
effort to win Christians over to Marxism, a
strategy which contrasted sharply with Herron's earlier effort to Christianize socialism.
More moderate reformers, such as Richard
T. Ely, Graham Taylor, Charles Sheldon,
William Jennings Bryan and Booker T.
Washington, reflected generally a more evangelical bias, as historians Charles Howard
Hopkins, Henry May, and the late Aaron I.
Abell noted over twenty years ago. The
steady advance of the idea of a Kingdom
of God in America among both socialists
and moderates eventually bore fruit in the
organization of the Federal Council of
Churches of Christ in America, and its adop-
tion from a previous Methodist statement
of the influential "Social Creed of the

Churches."

George D. Herron, however, remains for students of American history the symbol of the radical left wing of the Protestant social awakening. How radical was he? The sermons in this volume indicate that the rhetoric of the Kingdom Movement, certainly, and many of its ultimate convictions as well sprang from traditional and Biblical faith.

Here is no sentimental reconstruction of the social teachings of Jesus, no labored effort to turn the Sermon on the Mount into a crusader's call. Three of the six addresses take as their starting point incidents from the Old Testament which then, as now, held great fascination for tough-minded evangelicals: Abraham's near sacrifice of his son Isaac, Jacob's wrestling with his conscience through the long night before his reunion with Esau, and Elijah's bitter complaint against the people of Israel for choosing Baal over Jehovah. Two of the three sermons on New Testament themes rested upon Pauline texts, rather than the Gospels, and were powerfully theological. Only one in-

volved Jesus: Herron based his analysis of
the relationship between repentence and service upon the questions Jesus asked Peter at
the sea-side breakfast in Galilee, after the
Resurrection. The choice of text could scarcely
have pleased the *avant-garde* of contemporary
Biblical scholars.

The first of the six sermons, analyzing
Abraham's spiritual development at Moriah,
deals with love as a social force. By acting
out his willingness to sacrifice Isaac, Herron
said, Abraham enabled God to show him the
difference between making his son "an individualistic joy and the founder of a family"
and dedicating him to "the development of a
redemptive history." The patriarch discovered "that power is love, and that righteousness is simply love realizing itself through
sacrifice," a conviction which became thereafter the foundation of both Hebrew and
Christian ethics. "The socialization of love
is its life and growth," Herron declared,
"and is the ground upon which we are promised immortality." As Abraham on Moriah,
so Jesus at Calvary revealed the whole proc-

ess of creation to be "an eternal development of the life of God through sacrifice . . . the eternal becoming of God in obedience to the law of his being."

For these reasons, Herron said, sacrifice has been a central aspect of the religious consciousness in every culture. Christian love, however, goes beyond altruism. The latter bids individuals to act benevolently toward other individuals, whereas the "new man" the Gospel promises is "a social being fulfilling his life as a function of the social organism." Religious affections, therefore, "are not private property but social energies"; they are far more important than science in bringing about moral evolution. Once awakened to such emotions, Herron concluded, the Christian finds that "a pure socialism" is "the only form through which religion can express itself in life and progress."

The second address brings all of this to bear upon capitalism's rationalization of greed — what Herron calls "economic atheism." Jacob's religious life in exile had been like that of many modern businessmen, Herron declared: pious, but not ethical. He, like they, could excuse his many sins by claiming he had been "caught in a system of things" or that his selfish and quarrelsome wives had driven him to the feverish quest of wealth. Returning to the land of his fathers, however, Jacob could not escape an encounter with the brother whose birthright he had taken. Fear prompted him to send ahead to Esau as an act of restitution all that he possessed. Then, alone, he wrestled with God and his conscience until the break of day.

In similar fashion, Herron charged, religious words and rituals shielded nineteenth-century men of wealth from awareness of their "vast and continued resistance to God" and enabled them with a clear conscience to do "the strongest and most accursed wrongs." Great personal crises, however, might awaken their desire for moral renovation. Suffering could enable such men to discover "the social ground of religious experience" and to realize that they could not separate fellowship with God from righteousness in their "daily relations with men and things." Revival prayers, he declared, were of little value without the restoration of wealth gained through oppression or extortion. The holy man is "a whole man, normally fulfilling all the functions of his life," especially his responsibility for social justice. The professionally holy, he added, and especially the leaders of organized churches, had often taught the opposite view.

Herron's ethical emphasis here will seem novel enough to those who suppose nineteenth-century Christianity to have been narrowly Calvinistic, concerned more with divine election than with ethics or economics. But this sermon in fact bespoke the religion of William and Catherine Booth, whose evangelistic tours of American cities had recently been so successful. And it echoed the teaching of Methodist preachers who for three generations had opposed the pietist conception of holiness with a call to personal and ethical consecration. Charles G. Finney, in his *Lectures on Revivals of Religion* had precisely foreshadowed Herron's teaching sixty years earlier.

The contrast between Herron's version of Christian Socialism and the Marxist call for a revolution and dictatorship of the proletariat becomes clearly evident in the sermon on Elijah, entitled "The Leadership of Social Faith." Elijah's despair in the wilderness resulted from the individualism of his effort, from "the loneliness and mysticism that always mark the prophet." The "great man way" of making history, Herron declared, was out of date. At the present juncture in human affairs, a Luther would be a calamity, a Savonarola, a burden. The times required, rather, leaders who knew how to draw upon the inspiration of "the social faith of the peoples, the commonality of their moral feeling" and so bring in by love the Kingdom of equality. In a wildly romantic passage, Herron insisted that the "talk in the rude mining town, in the railroad construction camp, [or] on the mortgaged farms of the Dakotas," afforded "a clearer view of the social future of our nation than . . . economic or social science." What the common man's

"simple feeling for justice . . . says ought to
be," he declared, "is the authoritative word
of what will be." For this Christian and
Socialist, the voice of the people had become
the voice of God in a manner that would
have surprised Friedrich Hegel quite as much
as it would have amused Karl Marx.

The remaining three sermons are important chiefly for the theological implications
which they draw from the New Testament
and from the author's own social ideology.
The one dealing with Peter's denial and redemption makes a man's ignorance of his
sinfulness the greatest vice, and "the social
realization" of repentance the prime virtue.
To a Victorian generation, Herron declared
that redemption is far more important than
innocence; not a blameless life but a passion
for the increase of righteousness is the essence of Christianity. Such a redemption was
possible only for those who, in addition to
guilt for their individual evil, "felt the moral
pain and shame of all human life." Because
of their capacity for social feeling, he said,
"God has been obliged to make some of his

greatest saints out of greatest sinners." Their lives of service contradicted the "ethical skepticism" dominant among the nation's strictest churchmen, to whom "loveless spiritual pride, atheistic piety" and "religious unbelief in rightness" were habitual. These attributes, Herron declared, had received Jesus' unrestrained scorn. They were the antitheses of Christianity, however much they might reign in modern pulpits.

In the sermon on the unity of the material and the spiritual world, Herron pursued further the synthesis of romantic and socialist idealism which was implicit in his earlier comments on Elijah. Here he wove a magic carpet of social redemption from varied strands of neo-Hegelian pantheism, just as others, ranging from Christian Scientists on one hand to devotees of the Concord School of Philosophy on the other, had made that philosophy a way of personal salvation. In the new Kingdom, Herron said, "the material becomes spiritual, and the spiritual divinely material." Thomas Edison and Nicola Tesla were preparing the way of the lord quite as much as Martin Luther or Oliver Cromwell had done long before. Christian mysticism, transcendentalism, socialism, and applied science were for him the four horsemen of a new apocalypse, whose end would be the reign of justice and love.

Modern readers will find most provocative in this sermon the passage which announces Herron's readiness to "give up a philosophic absolute God." The death of that God, he declared, would result in "the gain of a Christian God" with whom men could hold "a human and social fellowship, having found him to be a Father, with feelings like the children who are his offspring." Faith in such a God, he added, underlay his belief in the physical resurrection of Jesus as well as his hope for personal immortality. When sin is at last banished from the earth, Herron prophesied, every relationship would be religious and "every human intercourse a social sacrament." Then death itself might disappear; for immortality stemmed from "the social spirit of the individual," from "the strength and reality of his love" and "the vitality of his relation to the social organism."

In the final sermon, however, Herron stood Hegel alongside St. Paul, and found the Apostle's philosophy of progress superior. For Paul recognized the social nature of evil as well as the power of social regeneration, whereas Hegel's touchstone was the individual's reach for personal transcendence. In a passage which anticipated what Walter Rauschenbusch later spelled out in *A Theology For the Social Gospel,* Herron reviewed the swiftly changing "scientific and popular attitudes toward the problem of evil and redemption." The story of Eden was no longer a joke, as it had seemed a few years previously, he said, "when evolutionary thought was young and exuberant, and many scientific discoveries were at hand." The "matchless narrative of the fallen" had become instead "the profoundest explanation of history possible to the inspired imagination." The Kingdom ideal of a perfect society did not rest upon the abandonment of the doctrine of original sin but upon the reformers' faith in the sanctifying triumph of God's love.

Such a doctrine was new only to the consistent Calvinism which still held sway at Princeton Theological Seminary. Popular preachers like Edward Beecher, Charles G. Finney, Gilbert Haven, Lyman Abbott, Horace Bushnell, and Matthew Simpson had been proclaiming a more progressive orthodoxy for half a century. The American Christian's passion for the sublime, as the late Perry Miller phrased it, had undergirded the movement for social reform before the Civil War. It also enlightened the effort to reconstruct national life on a radical basis after that desperate conflict ended. Herron's sermons reprinted here, and the Kingdom Movement he led, represented not so much a new ideology as a summing up of what James C. Malin has called the *Concern About Humanity* which had been for decades a distinguishing mark of nineteenth-century American evangelicalism. What was new was the young professor's readiness to state spiritual principles radically, and to apply them in a direct attack upon the capitalistic system at a moment when American Marxists were mounting their first major assault against it.

Timothy L. Smith

A SELECT BIBLIOGRAPHY

Source Materials

Bliss, William D. P., ed. *The Encyclopedia of Social Reform*. New York, 1897.

Gladden, Washington. *Christianity and Socialism*. New York, 1905.

Handy, Robert T., ed. *The Social Gospel in America; Gladden, Ely, Rauschenbusch*. New York, 1966.

Herron, George D. *Between Caesar and Jesus*. New York, 1899.

Herron, George D. *The Christian Society*. New York, 1894.

Herron, George D. *The Larger Christ*. New York, 1891.

Herron, George D. *The New Redemption: A Call to the Church to Reconstruct Society According to the Gospel of Christ*. New York, 1893.

Herron, George D. *The Christian State: A Political Vision of Christ*. New York, 1895.

North, Frank Mason, "The Christianity of Socialism," *Zion's Herald*, Vol. 69 (January 28, 1891), p. 25; and "Socialism and Christianity," *ibid.*, Vol. 69 (February 4,

1891), p. 34.

Tolman, W. H., and William J. Hull, *Bibliography of the American Institute of Christian Sociology* (2nd ed.; New York, 1893).

White, Eliot, "The Christian Socialist Fellowship," *Arena,* Vol. 41, no. 229 (January 1900), pp. 47–52.

Books and Articles

Dombrowski, James. *The Early Days of Christian Socialism in America.* New York, 1936.

Handy, Robert T. "George D. Herron and the Kingdom Movement," *Church History,* XIX (June 1950), 97–115.

Handy, Robert T. "Christianity and Socialism in America," *Church History,* XXI (March 1952), 39–54.

Hopkins, Charles Howard. *The Rise of the Social Gospel in American Protestantism, 1865–1915.* New Haven, 1940.

Reckett, Maurice B. *Maurice to Temple: A Century of the Social Movement in the Church of England.* London, 1947.

SOCIAL MEANINGS

OF

RELIGIOUS EXPERIENCES.

SOCIAL MEANINGS

OF

RELIGIOUS EXPERIENCES

BY

GEORGE D HERRON

A course of lecture-sermons prepared for the Settlement School of Social Economics, held by Prof. Graham Taylor, D.D., at Chicago Commons, August 22–29, 1895; afterward given in the Shawmut Congregational Church, Boston.

———

NEW YORK: 46 EAST FOURTEENTH STREET
THOMAS Y. CROWELL & COMPANY
BOSTON: 100 PURCHASE STREET

C. J. PETERS & SON, TYPOGRAPHERS.

To the Memory

OF

THE REV. JOHN P. COYLE, D.D.

CONTENTS.

I.

THE AFFECTIONS AS SOCIAL ENERGIES.

GEN. XXII. 1, 2.

PICTURE a household in which the mysteries of life are made plain, and its commonplaces transfigured in the light which is shed from those four poems in Luke's Gospel. Given the home of a Jewish carpenter, poor but not pinched, in sunny, flowery, free Galilee, with its synagogues, its Sabbath, its Scriptures, its annual pilgrimage to Jerusalem, its saturation to the point of precipitation with the ideas and sentiments which these institutions have been fostering for centuries. Give this family as its prime consciousness, no matter how come by, a conviction, perhaps not rare among pious households in that day, that it had in its bosom Him who was to fulfil the expectation of Israel; and let this conviction find its specific modes of conception in the shape of this maternal song now ascribed to Mary, this paternal song ascribed to Zacharias, this heart-song of the shepherds ascribed to the angels, and the sage words ascribed to the aged Simeon. Let the daily life be lived, the weekly Sabbath spent, the Scriptures repeated, the visits to Jerusalem made, and all these things find their interpretation, at least to the heart of yearning and brooding motherhood, in the terms of such poems as these, and what an atmosphere must have been generated in that home! The very presence of the Hebrew spirit, in its most religious and sacredest manifestation, as "the spirit of the holy gods," of the Holy One of Israel, the Holy Spirit, must have reigned in that home, nurturing the messianic character, and preparing a basis for the messianic consciousness of Jesus of Nazareth. — *John P. Ccyle*, in "The Spirit in Literature and Life."

THE wings of the soul lose their plumes; the leaves of the flower fast fall off and wither; and of this fountain of love there remain but a few drops. We still call these few drops love; but it is no longer the clear, fresh, all-abounding child-love. It is love with anxiety and trouble, a consuming flame, a burning passion; love which wastes itself like raindrops upon the hot sand; love which is a longing, not a sacrifice; love which says, "Wilt thou be mine?" not love which says, "I must be thine." It is a most selfish, vacillating love. And this is the love which poets sing, and in which young men and maidens believe; a fire which burns up and down, yet does not warm, and leaves nothing behind but smoke and ashes. — *Max Müller*, in "Memories."

SOCIAL MEANINGS OF RELIGIOUS EXPERIENCES.

I.

THE AFFECTIONS AS SOCIAL ENERGIES.

And it came to pass after these things, that God did prove Abraham, and said unto him, Abraham; and he said, Here am I. And he said, Take now thy son, thine only son, whom thou lovest, even Isaac, and get thee into the land of Moriah; and offer him there for a burnt offering upon one of the mountains which I will tell thee. — GEN. xxii. 1, 2.

IN the literature of national and religious beginnings, the most interesting and effective figure is that of Abraham. Whatever the scholars may decide as to dates and facts, we are sure that we have a true outline of the patriarch's life. The story is so artlessly beautiful, so divinely without design, that its lessons win and delight the moral reason. His

life does not belong to the heroic or Homeric
type, but rather to the idyllic, which is greater.
The character of Abraham is too simple and
natural, too true and morally majestic, to form
an epic. He was not a perfect man; he
sinned, sometimes, and blundered. But he
looms above his times, which were full of
both hideous decay and vast potency, as the
best offering that humanity for long ages could
make to God.

Abraham does not seem to have been interested in any particular form of religion, or to
have cared at all for religion as such; his
interest was in human life and its relations.
Over life's meaning and problems, its resources
and destiny, he was always brooding. Being
the man he was, he could do little else at
such a time. An old and wonderful civilization, about the power and triumphs of which
the records of books and bricks give us only
hints, was passing away; and Abraham felt
himself both called and driven to begin somewhere a new order of things. He was pursued by some sort of a social ideal, and

dreamed of a holy national life. His call never allowed him to be satisfied with what he had done, or with himself; he must always be seeking some better thing. Whenever he was overcome by suggestions to adjust his faiths and ideals to the seeming facts and forces of his life and environment, then the elements of moral tragedy and endless suffering entered his career. We read lightly the story of the sending away of Hagar into the wilderness, if we do not see in Abraham a terrible and helpless sufferer. His was the matchless suffering of needing to make another suffer, and that other the mother of his own child, for that which was in no sense her sin, but which was the guilt of his own hesitancy and unbelief. Worse than that, the sin and sorrow both came through her whose bidding he had in weakness obeyed in order that he might have peace. So every attempt to trust the fulfilment of his soul's promises to what our scientific age would call the facts of his life, rather than to the divine risk of that moral adventure which will follow no star but its own ideal, resulted in tragedy and failure.

But there were few such failures in Abraham's life. One trial of his faith nerved him for a greater. Each proof of his obedience strengthened him for another. He was a domestic man, loving his kinsmen and native country. But when, probably after years of increasing discontent with the existing Chaldean conditions of society, he was moved by that mighty and concluding impulse to get away into a distant country he had never seen, and there found a new nation, Abraham obeyed and entered upon the divine adventure. This was one of those commanding impulses which the Hebrew so simply and accurately called the word of God; which men have never been able to disobey without the loss of vision and spiritual reason, — the problems of life henceforth being figured out rather than seen through. God gave Abraham great possessions. But when a dispute arose between Lot's herdmen and Abraham's herdmen as to land and water rights, Abraham

at once surrendered the fairest of his lands
to one who had no just claim upon them.
He was more sensitive to the social honor
and peace than to his own rights; more anxious to keep the social faith, to preserve the
brotherhood, than to keep his possessions.
When his ungracious and selfish nephew was
carried away captive by a marauding king,
Abraham immediately gathered his friends,
and marched to Lot's rescue. On the eve of
Sodom's destruction we find him pleading with
God for the salvation of his sinning neighbors. Perhaps without knowing it, Abraham
treated his whole life as a social function,
to be used of God for all sorts and conditions
of men. His life is rich in ethical romance,
his career full of social chivalry. He was so
unfailingly the friend of man, that he came
to be known among neighboring tribes and
nations as the friend of God. So vital and
familiar was his fellowship with God, so strong
and faithful his search for what was good for
man, that God delighted to be Abraham's
guest, to come in and sup with him, and con-

fide to him the future. Through all his long pastoral life, increasing in sweet moral dignity and social value with each new experience, adversity and prosperity alike prepared him for whatever God might ask, and gave him a purer view of things to come. Like Isaiah and Socrates, with many of the good and wise men of the more anxious centuries that were to follow him, Abraham saw Christ's day and was glad ; just as we may see the perfected humanity and rejoice. When the call came to offer Isaac, Abraham was responsive to the call, long years of training in the school of obedience having prepared him to make this supreme sacrifice.

There came a time, so the story reads, when God would make proof of Abraham. The command is so worded that it becomes a sort of moral vivisection : "Take now thy son, thine only son, whom thou lovest, even Isaac, and offer him for a burnt offering." This was the son whom God had given him as one from the dead, after years of praying and patient waiting, as the beginning of a new and better people, whose numbers were to be as the sands of the sea. There must be both an immediate and an eternal worth to the lesson which God would teach Abraham through the agony and surrender, the triumph and peace, of such an experience. For we must keep in mind it was really Abraham, not Isaac, who was to be sacrificed; Abraham, not Isaac, who was to make the surrender of will, and the offering of life. We should also consider that it is not the soul unused to sorrow that feels a sorrow most keenly, as we are apt to think, but the soul that has been attuned to songs of grief by deep experience; sorrow alone prepares the heart to apprehend sorrow in the reality and fruitfulness of its meaning. Abraham's previous experiences could only sharpen the anguish of this strongest demand upon his faith. Yet Abraham walked trustfully to the altar upon which he was to offer his son to God. He did not seek to delay or evade strict obedience. He did not trifle with what he understood to be his duty; he juggled not with his conscience.

He did not tell Sarah, in order that she might dissuade him from his sacrificial pilgrimage, as she doubtless would have tried to do. His preparatory struggle lasted but a single night, and then he prepared to act ; not with sullen resignation, but with trustful and triumphant obedience. Isaac was already slain in Abraham's heart before he left his tents at Beersheba for the land of Moriah. The writer of the Epistle to the Hebrews suggests that Abraham accounted God able to raise Isaac from the dead, if such should be necessary to the fulfilment of the divine promise that Isaac should be the firstborn of a new nation. But it is not likely that the patriarch had any such thought, even after Isaac had already been offered in his heart. There is no indication that Abraham expected Isaac's restoration, or the provision of some substitutional sacrifice. Abraham was not playing hide and seek with God. His sacrifice was real, offered in the great faith that the righteousness which he could not then define, and could but vaguely understand, would some time be made intelligible to his moral sense.

The students of this event have already shown that the literal sacrifice and burning of Isaac's body need not have been a violation of Abraham's conscience. Human sacrifices were at that day the climacteric feature of the tribal and national religions. The chiefs and kings all about Abraham were accustomed to offer human beings as sacrifices to appease the wrath and gain the favor of their deities. From offering slaves and captives taken in war, they had come to offer their first-born sons — following the growth of the idea that the more valuable the sacrifice the better pleased was the deity. Of course Abraham could sacrifice as dearly to the God of all the earth as the chieftains and kings to their tribal deities, whatever the grief and cost, however long he must wait to know the righteousness of the sacrifice.

But God was able to enlarge Abraham's life, to light up both the retrospect and prospect of the Hebrew chieftain's career, without

the taking of Isaac's body. I think it is Dean
Stanley who states that the staying of Abraham's uplifted hand was forever afterward regarded by the Hebrew people as a protest
against human sacrifice. We know that among
ancient peoples the Hebrews are distinguished
for their sense of the sacredness of human life.
Frederick Robertson, with all his holy earnestness, protests against the common treatment
of the story as though Isaac were actually
slain by his father upon the altar. Yet these
miss the lesson of the sacrifice. The physical
life or death of Isaac was quite an incidental
matter, and should not so much exercise our
religious concern. It was Abraham, not Isaac,
who was being sacrificed ; Abraham's life, not
Isaac's body, that God was after. God did not
avert, but accomplished, the sacrifice by the
staying of Abraham's hand.

There was nothing arbitrary, even in the
best possible sense in which that word may be
used, in God's command to offer Isaac ; no
mere testing of the moral stuff of Abraham's
life. The sacrifice was not a divine deceit, but

was virtually made; not a trial and experiment, but a process and accomplishment; not a seeing if something could be done, but a doing of something. God does not do things because he can; nor does he try men to see what they are made of, as we often say. Trial is not fundamentally a probation, but an educative process, uniting man with his brothers and with God. It is not because God wants his own way that he leads us into the knowledge of his will along paths we walk with bleeding feet, through deeps of suffering, under billows of flame; but because only through his way can human life become social, and hence eternal. God calls for no sacrifice from man that he himself does not make for man; asks obedience to no moral law which does not organize his own activity; speaks nothing as truth for man that is not already truth in himself. The command to offer Isaac was given out of the fulness of God's faith in Abraham. It is an expression of both the delight and hope of God in our evolving and ascending human life; an expression of the joy which every growing man is to the heart of God. When Abraham offered Isaac in the faith that God was not only power, but that he would prove himself a righteous power, God not only gave him back a new Isaac, but a purer and vaster faith. In the course of this experience, Abraham dimly saw the Lamb eternally slain in the heart of God; that is, he saw, what the world yet scarcely dreams, that power is not merely righteous, but that power is love, and that righteousness is simply love realizing itself through sacrifice. Abraham came back from his adventure with a better future for the world on his hands, commissioned anew to care for the world's fundamental and final interests. The life of Israel, springing from Abraham, began with messianic impulses and a world movement stirring in its blood. On this parental tree grew the characters of Joseph, David, Elijah, Daniel, and the envisioned prophets. The character of Jesus is, in part, the fruitage of Abraham's faith. Jesus was the evolution of Hebrew national life and history, and without Abraham could not have been.

We get little of the lesson of Abraham's sacrifice from the empty exegesis of mere criticism, which lacks the prophetic sense and moral imagination, the vivid insight and historic spirit, essential to true interpretation. We are ethically degraded by the inane pietisms that are the staple of the religious commentaries; the most commonly relished of these pious comments on Abraham's sacrifice are not only immoral in substance, but socially vicious in application.

In general, the pietistic interpretations put God in the attitude of trying an experiment to see whether Abraham really loved him better than his son Isaac. Of course the idea always is, that Abraham was in danger of an idolatrous love for Isaac, and that he had to be shown this danger through the proposed sacrifice in order that he might give God the greater love. But the God of Abraham and Isaac, of Jesus and Paul, of Mazzini and Lincoln, is not the individualistic and unethical God he is pietistically conceived to be. God is not jealous of the love that unites human beings, but carries the cross in his heart to draw all men into eternal habitations of love. Love is the home of the normal man ; it is the Father's house, the natural social order, from which we have wandered prodigal, wasteful of life in our efforts to set up independent house-keepings. There was no balancing of quantities of love, to weigh out just how much Abraham should give to God and how much to Isaac. God was not trying an experiment, or anxiously trying to get a man to love him more than his son, but was evolving a character and commissioning a life.

The danger was not that Abraham should love Isaac too much, but that he should love him too little. The vast peril before Abraham, and before the purpose of God, was that Abraham's love for his son should dwindle into a mere individual and hence suicidal delight, and that both father and son should fall from the social function of their lives. The time had come when God would clearly show Abraham the difference between making Isaac an individualistic joy and the founder of a family, and

making his life a function in the development
of a redemptive history. The whole story
turns about the sacrifice of Isaac in service,
rather than in mere happiness or mere death.
This was the meaning of Abraham's sacrifice
of himself in the offering of his son Isaac;
this the new revelation that came to Abraham. These two men were sent upon a divine
errand. Their consciousness was not of an individual self to be gratified and delighted, but
of a human organism of which they were vital
and sustaining members. They saw a human
history to be made, a human destiny to be
wrought out, in which they were to be God's
organs. God was teaching Abraham the lesson the world is slowly learning from Jesus
and his cross, — the lesson that he that saveth
his life shall lose it, while he that loseth his
independent life to make it a function of the
common life finds it eternally. When Abraham was so wrought upon that he would surely
train his son to be an organ through which
God should work out a universal good, so
wrought upon that he could divinely risk his

son as an offering to God upon the altar of human need, then God could indeed say that he had a trustworthy friend in the man who withheld not his only son.

Speaking fundamentally, it is not science, but feeling, that makes for social evolution; and the affections are the social energies which are working out the unity and harmony of human life. Hence, before all else, the individual affections must be socially consecrated. The experiences of life are to teach us that love is social law, and not private property to be held for the gratification of one's self. Individual love is fulfilled only through becoming a social element. The individualization of love is a social disintegration, and is either the murder or suicide of love itself; the socialization of love is its life and growth, and is the ground upon which we are promised immortality. Delight in any human relation or affection chiefly for the happiness it brings to one's self is a perversion of love, and a reversion of the force that is working out the social evolution. Humanity is one body, of which

each individual life is a function; human society is one development, of which each individual is God's organ; human history has one
goal, to the reaching of which each individual
is consciously to consecrate himself as a living
member of the social body; human life has
one immortality, which is to be gained through
each individual affection becoming at last a
social energy. Only by lifting all human life
into the light and warmth, the power and fellowship, of one's highest and holiest love can
that love be sanctified and immortalized. He
is no true lover who is not willing to make his
love the moral property and social good of the
race; and, just as God does not want to be
loved apart from man, no righteous soul will
want to be loved apart from God and human
life. He who cares for a friend chiefly because
he can make that friend's life a continuous
contribution to his own enjoyment is not only
base and selfish; he is a traitor to his friend.
The exclusiveness of the affections is of the
devil, and issues in the works of the devil,
through the withdrawal of the richest and

strongest social forces from the sphere of their work. The best there is of us is social property, belonging to man as well as God; rather, belonging to God by belonging to man. Our affections, in every relationship of life, are Christian only as they are redemptive energies in the world. The loves of our hearts are pure only when they glorify humanity in our eyes. Our love for those with whom we hold the closest fellowship is unrighteous until we make it a power of God unto the social salvation. We dare isolate in thought no singularly noble soul, making the common life seem of low worth in the light that should make it glorious; for the glory of a great white soul is in the fact that it is a revelation of our one human life. Unless our affections are lifting us to the things that are above the delight of self, and are a power lifting the whole human life to the righteousness of Jesus, they but deepen the shadows of selfishness which so long hide the face of God from man.

The love which regards its nearest object as a social agent is the opposite of the feeling that searches for its object the ways of moral ease and physical comfort. There is much that shows the form and speaks the language of love that is without love's substance; much that passes for unselfishness that is really the cruelest selfishness — cruelest because it is the selfishness of weakness. In family, church, and state, we are easy with what we know to be wrong, with what is expedient or relatively right ; we fail of the living and unceasing sacrifice of upholding the divine ideals. What we are devoutly regarding as a love for others is a love of self, and a regard for our own moral ease. It makes us hypocrites towards our neighbors without their knowing it, and makes us the deceivers of our own selves.

The failure to discern between the love of self and the love of others is a mistake which Dr. Gladden makes in a recent discussion of "The Law of the Kingdom." "There are many parents in these days," he says, "whose altruism is carried to a dangerous excess. They love their children so much more than they love themselves that they humiliate and degrade themselves — weakening their authority, destroying their influence, and thus depriving themselves of all power to do any really good thing for their children." [1] Few men see as clearly, or speak as nobly and wisely, as Dr. Gladden. Yet what he calls a dangerous excess of love on the part of parents for their children is not parental love, but exactly the lack of love ; it is one of the most dangerous forms of selfishness, growing out of the worst and weakest self-love. The degrading fact with these parents is that they do not love their children ; they are making their children the mere functions of parental self-gratification, and the victims of parental moral indolence, instead of educating them for the social service. Such parents regard their own comfort of body and ease of mind, their pride and complacency, more than either the well-being of their children or the social good. There was once a mother whose child was caught for a number

[1] " The Church and The Kingdom," p. 68.

of hours in a cold rain, causing rheumatism which threatened to cripple the child for life. The physician, by every sort of persuasion and command, made the mother understand that unless she would often move the limbs and work the joints of the child, he would soon become rigid and helpless. After a few feeble attempts, the mother would not do, nor would she permit the nurse to do, as the physician had ordered. Her constant and pathetic plea was that she loved her child so much she could not bear to have him suffer the pain that came from obeying the physician's commands. The child became a cripple, and then, after two or three years of terrible suffering, died. Now, it was not her child the mother loved, but herself. She was guilty of the most miserable self-love, and was actuated by an inordinate regard for her own feelings rather than a regard for her child. In the ethical and social world, precisely the same sort of self-deceit and hypocrisy are masquerading as love. The selfish affection we are apt to call love is separative and disintegrating, exclusive and lustful, deadly and tyrannous, because it is love fallen from its true estate.

This perversion and apostasy of love, so current in modern social life, is sending from our homes, churches, and schools, young men and women untrained in even the first principles of social right and wrong. Even the most religious of us are without ethical sense regarding human relations. The want of such a quality of love in the home, and such a knowledge of Jesus' teachings in the pulpit, as will make our young men and women ethically intelligent, so that they may know social right in distinction from social wrong, is the most foreboding feature of American life and religion. Parents who suffer their children to grow up in social ambition, dominated by the principles that make a virtue of covetousness and glorify a career of absorbing self-interest, should be taught that they are the destroyers of their children, and social traitors as well. The affections are not private property, but social energies. The social responsibility of the affections can be unknown or ignored only at the peril of both giver and receiver. Yet with nothing — not with material gains — are we so selfish and perverse, so individualistic and suicidal, so destructive to human life, as with our affections.

This has its sequence in the wretched fraudulency that parades itself in the political arena as patriotism and party fealty; or, again, in the religious self-deceit which so anxiously exhibits itself as loyalty to the church, but which is in effect the subtlest and wickedest treason to the church. He who ought to know the evil in his household, his country, his church, and yet chooses to ignore it, making not his life a vicarious sacrifice to bear it away, may think that love is the principle of his imagined good-will. But this good-will of his is the mask of a cruel hypocrisy, which God strips off before his nobler brothers at the judgment day of some great crisis. When one fails to commit himself to the highest ideal of right he knows, out of regard for the physical, social, or religious comfort of those he loves, he is at that moment false to those to whom he seems to be true. Frederick Robertson well said that, "he who prefers his dearest friend to the call of duty, will soon show that he prefers himself to his dearest friend."

The social responsibility of love cancels any warrant for limiting our relations. The new religious experience which the social conscience is giving us will deliver love from ascetic abandonments, as well as individualistic perversion by the pursuit of happiness. That love endures and grows only through fulfilling a social mission, and hence bearing within itself a vicarious sorrow, is only a recreant's reason for not loving. Not less, but more unselfish, love is the remedy for the evils of self-seeking affection. To limit and sever our human fellowships, rather than bear their responsibilities, is weakness and infidelity. As sons of God, it is of our moral errantry to accept human faiths and affections, with all the accumulating responsibilities and sacred sorrows they bring, and make them the power by which we shall be crucified to self; then we may rise with those we love into the social glory of the kingdom of Christ. Abiding in his quality of love, in the secret places of the Father's heart, where flows eternally the cleansing blood, there we may have given us all power in heaven and on earth to keep his commandment to love one another as he loved his friends. This love will see in every human life a brother, an eternal child of the heavenly Father, and will be intent upon presenting all whom it infolds white and whole for the redeemed society. It will express itself in a passion of service for the unloved and the unloving, and be as free from every impurity as the breath of angels. For itself it will not speak; nor seek its own joy; nor be tainted with the bitterness of loss; nor murmur at what God may give against desire; nor grow weary in waiting for the gates of life to open; nor feel baffled at work amidst unrequiting selfishness, knowing that it obeys the law by which all selfishness shall at last be overcome.

There is no short road to Moriah, and no one can take it in our stead. The journey stretches into days, or months, sometimes years. But until, with Abraham, we have become consciously caught in the world movement, and have been with him to Moriah, to sacrifice our life through offering the dearest objects of our affections upon the altar of the social service, neither we nor those we love are fitted to be full partakers of the salvation of our God, and of the authority of his Christ. When Jesus conditioned discipleship in his school of righteousness on a love for himself greater than love for father or mother, brother or sister, wife or children, it was not that his disciples should love these less, but love them more. This was no individualistic demand on Jesus' part for an affection for himself, but a call for supreme devotion to himself as the living incarnation of the idea of the righteous society. It was the fundamental necessity of discipleship that all relations should be ordered with a view to realizing the kingdom of heaven on the earth, — each individual discipleship be-

coming a social function, and each affection
a social energy. We never love righteously
until we are ready to stand by the cross of
our loved ones, as God stood in the shadow
of the cross of his Son; until we love our
sons and daughters because they lay down
their lives for the sheep. The most glorious
career that love can conceive for its object is
one of complete sacrifice in the service of the
common life. The affections will realize the
love from whence they spring by constraining
every loved one to become consecrate to bearing away the sins of the world, knowing that
to choose safety while our brothers are in peril
is to gain perdition, and that to endure stripes
and pain for the social healing is to receive the
life and peace of the Christ, when he cometh
in the fulness of his kingdom.

Centuries after Abraham, a holier lesson
than his was taught by a closing experience
of Jesus' life. As he stood, on the last evening, in the gate of his death, his thoughts
and feelings were mastered by a love for the
friends who had continued with him in his

temptations and divine failures. While he talked with them, there seems to have swept before him a sort of universal vision of things to come. Looking down the years, he saw how much slower than he had first expected would be the redemption of man, and his growth in the righteous society. He had expected a national redemption, with a glorious world mission for his people, which he had been unable to accomplish because of their unbelief. This expectation he had yielded gradually, month by month, and it was torn from his heart with a grief greater than he could speak. The fate inevitable to his nation, having rejected its messianic man and opportunity, stood out before him, its most ardent patriot, and with it the travail and birth, the blessing and curse, of a new religion. In the long prospect was the growth of this religion, losing its early gladness and virility as it gained patronage and organization; passing into successive perversions of all he had taught or had in mind; making religion the end of man, rather than man the end of religion. It would repeatedly stand for all the things his soul had stood against, — the foe of his truest friends, the friend of his truest foes. Institutionalized faith would become the historic persecutor of the really believing. The righteous society must realize itself through apostasies and tyrannies, religious wars and reformations, orthodox atheisms and outcast truths. While any evil remained among men, so long as the economy of redemption should need to last, the faithful to his ideal must have the greatest sufferings and conflicts. An intense momentary longing seems to have come to him to take his questioning and baffled friends away from the immediate reach of evil, and from the sorrow of vicarious living. But to withhold them from redemptive participation in the world's wrong would be to fail in his own faith, and keep from them the life he had come to give. Perfect sacrifice had made his life holy ; not in their steads, but that they also might be made holy through sacrifice in the fullest service. In committing those most deeply embosomed in his affections to the law and ideal of his own life, while knowing that wrong invested with authority would visit its worst revenges upon them, Jesus filled up the measure of his own sacrifice, and kept his own faith unbroken.   This purest of moral triumphs can be best understood by those who, through like experience, have learned joyfully to commit whom they would protect to whatever destiny may issue from the sacrifice of service.

In the experience of Abraham with God and Isaac is also livingly written a simple yet full philosophy of sacrifice.   We cannot rid ourselves of the word and fact of sacrifice in life, religion, and progress.   We shall not have done with the word until we know its meaning and obey its truth.   "What good thing have my brothers," asked Buddha, "that did not come from search and strife and loving sacrifice?"   The race has found its ascending way, step by step, in the light of the fires of its martyrs.   He who is most consciously caught in the world movement,

and best fulfils his life as a function therein,
most surely walks the path that rises by
the way of Calvary. Upon those who wear
the dignity of divine sonship, and give out the
virtue of the healing joy, may be seen the
marks of moral tragedy. And the way of
sacrifice along which the race toils to its divine destiny — a way of toil and suffering
because it has been a way of sin — is tracked
with the blood of the feet of the Almighty.
When Jesus taught the renunciation of self as
the law of human growth, when he pointed
to the cross as the gate to life and freedom, he brought forth something which had
been wrought out in the experience of God.
There is a sense in which God grows, and
grows through giving his glory to his creation. The universe is, in fact, an eternal
development of the life of God through sacrifice ; it is the eternal becoming of God in
obedience to the law of his being.

In the universal religious consciousness,
sacrifice has been the great fundamental fact.
The primitive and ethnic idea of sacrifice

was always that of setting something apart
as pleasing unto the deity, to be offered to
him upon the altar; but at the heart of
even the most monstrous offerings was always present the notion that the sacrifice
effected human welfare.   In Hebrew sacrifices the redemption and ethical idea had
larger place and growth than in the ethnic
religions, but not without perversion.   Religious perversion has persistently conceived
sacrifice to be a substitute for righteousness.
In essence and ethic the theological conceptions of sacrifice are as monstrous and
immoral as the rudest and cruelest ethnic
conceptions; they are not only not different, but are historically and ethically the
same, the old tribal and pagan conceptions
of sacrifice surviving in modern theological
terms.   The notion of the sacrifice of one
as constituting a substitute for the righteousness of others, whether baldly expressed,
or unconsciously accepted by religious experience, is the curse of both religion and
society; it lies at the heart of the false com-

mercial integrities, the social hypocrisies and tyrannies, the political corruptions and legalized anarchies, committed by the religious.

Ethically and Christianly, sacrifice is love offering a holy life upon the altar of the common need. In reality, sacrifice is the eternal definition of righteousness. A better knowledge of Jesus, of God, and human life, will finally teach us, what we ought long ago to have learned, that no life is conceivably righteous that is not purposely lived for the common good ; that no life is to be thought of as Christian that is not made sacred for the social service, and thus fully sacrificed in bearing away the sins of the world.

Then it is not a divinely forced circumstance, but the simplest and most orderly proceeding, that we should be taught in a lesson of sacrifice the social function of the affections. By nothing else than perfect sacrifice can the affections be realized or understood. Sacrifice and affection are one and the same fact, as we shall one day learn ;

and society, in its last analysis, in its full realization, is nothing else than the organized
love of the people in obedience to the law
ɔf sacrifice.

This is not altruism, by which is meant
man as an individual struggling for the good
of other individuals ; it is man as a social
being fulfilling his life as a function of the
social organism, as a living member of the
one social body.   Once committed to sacrifice
as the fundamental fact of religion, as the
law of human growth, a pure socialism becomes the only form through which religion
can express itself in life and progress.   And
religion becomes superstition and tyranny, with
metaphysical definition and political degradation following, when not translated into terms
of social values, and manifested in social
justice.

Save through the apprehension of sacrifice
as the law of social and universal gravity,
human justice and peace, order and harmony,
are a dream never to become fact.   Recon-
ciliation to this law, as the organizing and

administrative law of our life and its institutions, is the world's sabbath of social rest,
which we have not yet entered because of the
hardening of our hearts with the evil of unbelief, but which we shall finally enter, to
make progress thenceforth in peace and not
in strife. Into the social sabbath, where all
the promises of justice will at last be fulfilled
in a social body that shall take from each according to his powers and give to each according to his needs, where a glory greater than
the visions of the prophets awaits the common
life, and a joy that hath not entered yet the
heart of man, the race will be led by a divine
spirit of moral adventure, which shall put life,
with its dearest and all, on the altar of a
perfect and living sacrifice to the world's social redemption and destiny. The men and
women in whom this spirit shall become fully
and vicariously incarnate will be so caught in
the world movement, and so charged with messianic forces, that to fall back into the pursuit
of individual happiness would be to them the
worst possible torment; they will put the

social wisdom and power of sacrifice to tests so true and practical that every mind shall at last understand, and every knee bow to acknowledge the dominion and glory of the law by which Jesus saves and reigns.

II.

ECONOMICS AND RELIGION.

Gen. xxxii. 24-29.

HE loved money, because the man who does not love money is a Socialist, and a Socialist is a Nihilist, and a Nihilist is an Atheist. And an Atheist is a man who has no religion. Therefore, the love of money being the root of all religion, he loved money because he was a religious man.

He loved it with a humble, tranquil veneration of its majesty, recognizing it gratefully as the sheet-anchor of that respectability which, to him, represented the good ship of state. To Cornelia it was merely a source of personal enjoyment — either of what you yourself possessed, as manifested, for instance, in the purchase of pine-apples — or of what your neighbors lacked, as exemplified when your pine-apples were bigger than anybody else's. To Hendrik it was a wondrous beneficent Omnipotence, enthroned in all that is not only great, but also good, the enemy of the improper, the improvident, the tattered, the discontented, in a word, the one tangible bulwark against the chaos of the anti-cosmos. He could not have reasoned it out, perhaps; but to him and his co-religionists the god of the Cosmos, its originator and its upholder, was gold. He was not altogether unreasonable, surely. The original King may have been Love, but his subjects have deposed him. — *Maarten Maartens*, in " God's Fool."

FOR as their religion, so their cross, is very gaudy and triumphant: but in what? In precious metals and gems, the spoil of superstition upon the people's pockets. These crosses are made of earthly treasure, instead of teaching the hearts of those who wear them, to deny it: and like them, they are respected for their finery. A rich cross shall have many gazers and admirers: the mean in this, as other things, are more neglected. I could appeal to themselves of this great vanity and superstition. Oh! how very short is this of the blessed cross of Jesus, that takes away the sins of the world! — *William Penn*, in " No Cross No Crown."

48

II.

ECONOMICS AND RELIGION.

And Jacob was left alone; and there wrestled a man with him
until the break of day. And when he saw that he prevailed not
against him, he touched the hollow of his thigh; and the hollow of
Jacob's thigh was strained, as he wrestled with him. And he said,
Let me go, for the day breaketh. And he said, I will not let thee go,
except thou bless me. And he said unto him, What is thy name?
And he said, Jacob. And he said, Thy name shall be called no more
Jacob, for thou hast striven with God and with man, and hast prevailed. — GEN. xxxii. 24–29.

In nothing is there more of both delight and
help than the way in which the Hebrew, with
his strong prophetic imagination, and according to that simplicity and wonder with which
he regarded the natural world, tells of his
religious struggles and impulses in terms of
the objective and pictorial.

Like that of Jesus' temptation in the wilderness, the story of Jacob's wrestling is a vivid
objectified description of a fateful subjective
experience, towards which all past experiences

had been converging, out of which were to issue vast destinies. We need not materialize the scene in order to translate it into the language of our common need. The struggle was real enough, gathering the tendencies of a nation's life, as well as the moral fate of the man himself, into the agony of a single night. The night wrestling of man with man by Jabbok ford puts before us the decisive conflict between God and self in Jacob's life, with God as victor, and evil stripped of its religious disguise. Jacob emerged from the crisis a new man with a new name. He was no longer Jacob the supplanter, but Israel the prince of God. The disposition to live with God independent of his relations to men was now subjected to the effort to live with God in and through his relations. In the moral heat of the struggle, the poison of Cain was purged from the Hebrew's life.

Through his previous years Jacob had been a religious man, worshipping God as he knew him, his life doubtless moving on a higher plane of conduct than the average life in neighboring tribes. In the way that seemed practicable, considering the manner of world in which he lived, he had thought himself a servant of God. I take him to have been up to this crisis much such a character, in his relation to his times, as the average Christian who now succeeds in business. He had been a scheming and grasping man of affairs, chiefly intent upon his material prosperity, crediting his large gains to the special favor of God, and appropriating religion as a contribution to his individual career.

According to current ethics, much might be said to justify Jacob's course, and even to make him an exemplary character, — such a one as we would call to preside over religious conventions, and glorify as a providentially reared benefactor. His business relations were with an idolatrous world, and he was caught in a system of things. If he tried to deal with men according to the righteousness that haunted his dreams, would he not lose the accumulations of his thrift, and the Lord thus lose his gifts ? Then his wives were hard to

get along with, — selfish, ambitious, quarrelsome. Above all, he was religious ; and how
injudicious and unreasonable it would be in us
to go measuring piety by financial methods in
so influential a man, likely at any time to have
money to give to our benefactions and institutions !

Still, Jacob was not satisfied. Neither was
God. The man could not rid himself of the
feeling that God was disappointed in his life,
and without pleasure in his career. This
mutual dissatisfaction brought about the experience by Jabbok ford. Having over-reached
Laban, his father-in-law, in Mesopotamia, he
had stolen away with his family, his servants
and herds, and likely what else he could lay
hands on, to come into the land of his father,
Isaac, from which he had fled from the wrath
of his brother Esau, whom he had defrauded,
twenty years before. The pursuit of Laban,
a dread of the revenge of his wronged brother,
a deepening sense of the separateness of his
life, all gave God an opportunity to press
close upon Jacob's soul. When reaching the

Jordan, he remembered that he had passed over it, at the beginning of his career, with no possession but his staff; now he was returning with a rich caravan. The unchanging goodness of God contrasted mightily with his own faithlessness. " I am not worthy," he confessed to the Lord, " of the least of all thy mercies, and of all the truth which thou hast showed unto thy servant." Whether he had heard of his warlike brother's feats of arms, or whether he was over-wrought with the fear which the unknown always begets in a soul consciously parleying with God, he knew that some profound moral change was required of him. As he considered his great increase of wealth, still taking it to be the gain of a specially favoring Providence, there mingled with his gratitude an agony of remorse. Rude as was his moral sense, this grandson of Abraham had in him enough of his ethical inheritance to be deeply conscious that something was wrong about his possession of this wealth. Somehow, there seemed to come over him an indefinable sense of the ethical incongruity of thanking God for having so providentially helped him to cheat and steal. He did not live at a time when, by giving a trifle from his robberies to endow a university, he could un-wittingly make such a clear revelation of the moral apostasy of religion as to enable him to think highly of himself. So he was caught in the characteristic Hebrew conviction that there is no ground for forgiveness for the past, no assurance for the future, save in the largest possible restitution for wrong-doing. For years God had been hard pursuing Jacob to this point, and now the decisive conflict was come. The shame of the past, now a threatening cloud over the future, intensified the solitude of the Syrian night, in which the soul of God, in the person of a man, met Jacob's soul in moral battle. Deny or ignore, forget or sophisticate, work how he would, down in the deeps of his being he had known better than his way of living. The hand that now held him in this crisis and peril had repeatedly smitten his conscience with fearful blows that would not heal. He had often overthrown the pursuing sense of wrong, only to be sternly laid hold of again by this hand, and brought face to face with the actual truth about himself. Evade as he would, put off as he would, the judgment time came at last, bringing him face to face with the ethical realities of his life, his soul naked to his own gaze.

The wrestling of Jacob was no religious ecstasy, no mysterious experience, but was grounded in financial transactions. He wrestled with the question of what to do with his accumulations of wealth ; shekels and camels were component elements of his agony. The story is set in an economic problem ; it is essentially an economic revelation. Clearly, when read historically, it was wrong relations with his fellow-men that formed the subject of Jacob's experience. He had been trying to be religious, to be God's servant, by making his religion an individualistic relation to God, — a relation to God apart from his relations to man. He was squeezed into moral plasticity between the finished pursuit of his wife's father and the anticipated attack of his brother. It was a man who wrestled with him until break of day ; not God apart from man, nor a demigod. He prevailed with God through prevailing with man, or prevailed with God in man ; he gained the blessing of God in gaining the blessing of man. Nothing more distinctly discloses the social ground of religious experience than this story of Jacob's wrestling.

That God seeks man is the first fact of religion. God wants from man an intelligent intimacy with his thought ; a conscious oneness with his purposes and work ; a close abiding in his affections ; a fellowship with the realities of his being. The soul of God sorrows to make itself understood, while his heart hungers for human sympathy. The Father longs to share all he is and has with sons who will know and love. As one of the early Christian writers used to repeat, " God has a need and craving for thee, having made thee divine for his glory." The

Bible is a record of God's progressive disclosure of himself in man. The fellowship of God with man revealed in Jesus is the point to which the older scriptures ascend, and from which the newer scriptures proceed. The picture which the Old Testament presents is always one of God visiting man, often without man's seeking. Abraham is God's friend and confidant, whom God sends into a far country to found a new nation, Hebrew history thus beginning in the intimacy of God with a man. God appears to question in his mind whether he ought not to confide to his friend Abraham the secret of the judgment he is about to visit on Sodom. Jacob, when leaving the old home to make a new, dreams of a ladder between heaven and earth, witnessing to the one reality of the two, with the angels of God climbing up and down. From Abraham to Jesus, through the course of development from Moses to David, in the visions and labors of the prophets, God draws closer to man in each new development, at last to behold the image of himself, the moral glory of his being, in the Son of his love. In Jesus, God gains that oneness with man which he sought back in the experiences of Abraham and Jacob; that oneness which is the human goal, and which can alone satisfy the Father with his sons.

That man seeks God is the second fact of religion. Human progress has been a quest on the part of man for harmonious and working relations with God. In the deeps of our being, we feel that there is a perfect righteousness, an eternal harmony, a strifeless and endless progress, for which we have been created; which we shall at last apprehend and have peace. The most occupied of men, those with the strongest lusts of money or flesh, with the greatest intellectual or religious greeds, have some continuing sense of being away from home, while seeking home by ways that lead them farther from their destination. The divine unrest of life brings us all to camp by Jabbok fords every night, where we are harassed by the discord of our relations with our brothers and with God, when we have planned to be left alone. In the lone midnight hour, in the crowded street, in the counting-room, in the student's quarters, we are in ceaseless pursuit of God when we know it not; when we least expect it, we stumble upon burning bushes where God waits us. The quest of God, whom no man by mere searching hath found out, has been alike the joy and the tragedy of our human evolution.

This search has its living, though misread, inspiration in what Frederic Harrison calls the "ascendency of simple goodness" in both historical and personal crises. The princes of God are always mightier and more feared, and thus likely to be taken for public enemies by institutions and authorities, than the supplanters, whose foundations the princes dig away for the foundations of the holy society. When a soul feels the touch of God, it takes on something of God's moral dignity. To one who hears and heeds the whispers of God, he gives a sense of his own responsi-

bility, with that unmeasured authority over
men and things which so empowered the
souls of the prophets and apostles. Though
the life in which God has prevailed is profoundly humble, it is yet conscious that God's
almightiness belongs to it, and moves upon
its mission as though the destinies of the
earth depended upon its effort — as they do.
The wisest sage, the strongest warrior, the
cunningest accumulative merchant, resist as
each may, feels foolish and helpless in the
presence and power of a real saint's white
soul. No measure has ever been found to
man's capacity for righteousness; no reckoning to the moral might which God may
manifest in human life through a single soul.
Even in those classed worthless, we are
always catching glimpses of potential saint-
hood; the stupid and ignorant, hedged in by
the most difficult environment, become ethical
marvels, spiritually messianic. "The majesty
of goodness" is both more sovereign and
potent in the common life than the prudent
and strong know.

But between this seeking of God for man and seeking of man for God is a vast and continued resistance to God on the part of man. By every device the evil genius of self-will can conceive, both religious and openly rebellious, we seek to evade coming to close quarters with God ; we try to hide from our eyes the ethical realities of our life. We are willing to worship ; to believe the doctrines commonly accepted by organized religion ; to support a clergy and be benevolent ; to be devoutly pious, so far as anything may be required of us by the church ; to conduct our life according to profitable moral codes current ; to be full of the integrity that accrues from the precious fictions of economic laws. But our real career is apt to be a living prayer to the good Lord to deliver us from actual obedience ; while the history of official religion is largely the record of organized substitutes for righteousness. We make life a game of hide and seek with God. Knowing our wrong, feeling God's hard pursuit, through long years we put off the decisive conflict, looking for a salvation of circum-

stances to take the place of a salvation of
obedience ; hoping that God will interpose by
yet unforeseen events, send fearful suffering
even, — for we would all rather suffer than
obey, — to take from us the moral responsibility of decision.   We do not mean this hide
and seek with God as rebellion.   But rebellion
it is of the subtlest and fatalest sort, — a persistent demand upon God for quarter, instead
of a loving acceptance of his will as our meat
and drink.

The worst result of this resistance is ethical
insanity ; and the worst of this insanity is its
unquestioning belief that it is sane.   It is thus
that the world may go straight to perdition
under the guide of what we are pleased to term
a clear conscience.   The genius of evil knows,
what the average religious man ignores, that
sincerity may be no indication of righteousness.   Cruel and blind bigotry, and the idle
and commonplace vices, may be alike sincere.
Detestable moral juggling, graceless ethical
sophistry, social oppression and iniquity, all
stalk among men in the cloak of conscientious-

ness, wearing the solemn or smiling face of sincerity. The hardest fact of evil to be dealt with is the clear conscience with which the strongest and most accursed wrongs are done. If there is such a part of man's ethical being as our immoral moral sciences call conscience, it is none the less true that the conscience is a safe guide only when God is the guide of the conscience. Conscientiousness may be in no wise righteousness.

Yet there are terrible awakenings from the darkness of our clear consciences ; there is an ethical insanity that discovers itself to be not sane, and through this discovery comes a fearful return to our moral senses. This accounts for the close relation of great moral developments to great sufferings. Though God sought Jacob in a time of extremity, hours passed before the self in Jacob was overcome. While Paul's revelation of truth was abundant beyond his power to disclose, by some unrevealed pain or shame he was kept humble. Peter was a human rock on which Jesus might build ; but Peter dared not forget the floods of passion which sometimes swept him far away from the foundation in which he was laid. Even when we know we are parleying with God, our controversies with him we do not quickly settle. God has to wound and bruise, strain our thighs and stick thorns in our flesh, tear up deep roots of self-will, wrench our affections until each moment is a condensed eternity of pain, before we become plastic in the divine mould. Like Jacob, we have to be squeezed into moral plasticity between vanishing and awaiting extremities. In the social organism it takes a Spanish Inquisition to usher in religious freedom, and a French Revolution to translate this into political freedom ; God knows what it may yet cost to translate both into the freedom of economic equality !

But in the midst of this long resistance, with the pain and waste it brings, is the perverted seeking after God, which is the worst fact of historical religion. Though perverted seeking be but a disguised or unconscious resistance, the element of perversion is vaster and deeper than the element of positive resistance. Jacob's trouble was a wrong or un-social seeking of God, rather than a direct disobedience; a quest of God as power, rather than a seeking of God as righteousness. Our common trouble is the quest of God in the terms of religion rather than in the terms of actual life. We search for God independent of the human facts with which we are in daily touch, and which are the fund of life's real experience.

The logic of the search for God in religious rather than social terms is the priestly conception of religion, as certainly modern as it is heathen, and Protestant as well as Roman and Greek, always depending upon mysteries between God and man. The theological metaphysics which supports religion as a thing in itself, as a cult of worship, rather than an organization of right relations, are the ancient mysteries in modern forms. God hates mystery; while in religious mystery selfish man revels, as he cultivates perplexity in economics, because he thereby escapes social duty. Mystery in religion, with its theological or ecclesiastical priesthood, is the one sure ground of the tyranny of wealth and of corruption in the state. It is thus wholly logical that monopoly now swiftly tends, as it is everywhere tending, to the support of ecclesiasticism and theology. That official religion should first forget, then hold in disrepute, the religion of social aspiration and human fact, is the natural development of religious mystery into economic tyranny and social anarchy.

Religion is not the dispensation of any priesthood, either ecclesiastical or theological, one of which is as evil to society as the other. No set of men can control the course of God's righteousness in human life, nor monopolize the Holy Ghost. God breathes his Spirit on whom he pleases, being pleased with all who hunger and thirst after righteousness; and we cannot tell whence that Spirit cometh or whither it goeth. Obedience to the highest right and fullest service they know, is the organ of God's larger revelations of himself to men. His sweetest messages are not written in books nor spoken by priests. God gives his strength to human weakness by modes simpler than the thought of man can comprehend or the words of man express. Service is the language of the soul, by which soul speaks to soul on earth ; by which the soul of God speaks to the soul of Jacob and Paul, to your soul and mine. It is no part of the religious experience of the prophets and apostles of Jesus which enthrones God in an infinite nowhere, there in an eternal fret about what we conceive to be his own glory, approachable chiefly in terms of theological definitions, ordinances of worship, or religious organizations. One may have true and clear opinions about God, and express them in strict and reputable forms of worship, yet be withal the more infidel, even atheistic. In the realm of righteousness, nothing is more colossally impudent than that the people should be told what to believe by religious monopolies, which distract the world in trials of men for heresies on questions of Hebrew philology, or refuse to trust the message of redemption with men who think too ethically or hopefully of the

Son of God; and this, while ecclesiastically
ignorant of the great problems of right and
wrong bearing a chosen nation to a fearful
crisis, if not catastrophe. Considering his
times and training, Nero fiddling while Rome
burned is not a more shocking moral spectacle.

The chief characteristic of Biblical religion,
from Moses to Jesus, is the revelation of
God in the simplest facts of the common
life, in the terms of social effort. Fellowship with God is Scripturally disclosed in
anything but occult or mythological modes,
mysterious or theological terms. Both the
legal and prophetic revelations of the Old
Testament are in terms always sociological,
and but incidentally theological; in forms
distinctly political, having to do with social
conditions and political outlooks. Moses has
revelations concerning sanitary laws, architec-
ture, marriage relations, land ownership, good
government, and the commonwealth of society. Elijah and Isaiah, with all the prophets,
are social and national reformers. David is
a man of affairs, and Ezekiel a teacher of

political ethics. Jesus is simply reared, a carpenter by trade, and seems to live the most domestic of lives in his parental home and among his friends. His teachings or doctrines have to do with human relations, and are more distinctly economic than what we understand by the term religious. His ideal is social, and his work to redeem men for the righteous society called the kingdom of heaven. He reveals the relation of God to man in the simplest movements of nature, in the ordinary tasks of the common life, in the most explicit terms of economic communism. Christianity comes from him, not as a theological or ecclesiastical system, but as a revelation of life; not as a cult of worship, but as a social ideal, to be realized in a human order in which all shall live for the common good.

The social ground of religious experience is then a fundamental fact of religion. We cannot hold fellowship with God apart from the particulars of our occupation and career, apart from our daily relations with men and things. Religious experiences outside the terms of work and fact are a fiction and an evil, leading men and religion astray, and leaving human life unredeemed in the hands of its enemies. We know the legend that Julian the emperor once said that it is much easier to worship Jesus than to obey him. Whether the saying be Julian's or not, it is true in Christian history and experience. It is easy to be worshipfully or professionally religious; to be just and righteous is quite another matter. Religion is relations; and a right relation with God is primarily a right relation with human life, where the God of man is. The social fruit of individual religious experience is its value alike to God and man; it is without value except it change and ethically glorify the actual facts of life.

The religious, because social, test of life is in the quality of our relations with men of all sorts and conditions. This test comes to us amidst our work in the school, the factory, the mine, the workshop, the farm; amidst the highly respectable dishonesties of the counting-room, and the wretched integrities of commercial conceit; amidst the average pastorate, where sweet religious lies become habitual before recognized, destroying both intellectual and ethical manhood, and often putting a reputable moral emaciate in the place of a man; amidst home experiences, which are the social fountain, and where our lives falsify all our ideals. That the banker does not open his bank in the morning with the doxology, that the legislation of the state is not worded in religious phraseology, that the carpenter does not saw off each board with the Lord's Prayer, that the merchant does not dismiss his customers with the benediction, that the judge does not convene court with chapters from Leviticus, that the insurance company does not print the Sermon on the Mount in its policies, renders these operations none the less social sacraments and rituals of justice; they are all religion. Whoever casts from his bank door, or barn door, or factory door, or club-house door, or political-caucus door, or ball-room door, or kitchen door, the social shrine, is so far an atheist. For atheism is God-out-ness from life ; and religion is God-in-ness in life, making every human act and intercourse a religious rite.

The judgment of the social test no true religious experience can doubt. To be morally splendid in the heat of public conflict, in the thick of controversy and joined battle, eve.i in martyr-fire or dungeon chain, is easier than to fulfil the sacrifice of service with the things and duties in hand. "It is strange," said Mazzini, "but true, that men who are ready, if need be, to shed their blood for liberty, yet shrink from that pecuniary sacrifice by which that blood might often be spared." A small and often deceitful matter it is to become a leader of religion, to endow great philanthropies, to be known and honored by the successful ; it is the fulfilment of the plain career as a social function that best makes life a glory of God. The faith that removes mountains, that produces sheltered and protected religious devotees, that gives bodies to be burned for truth's sake, is not so great as the faith that loves the unloving and unlovable, and glorifies God by making the commonest tasks reveal him. The work given us to do is the altar of our approach to God, and the way we do it our worship.

That ours is a world of fact and toil, with the gulf between the ideal and the real greater than the purest and strongest seem able to pass, I do not forget. To the truest and bravest, life often proves a school of slow and sad disenchantment. There is bread to earn, it is true, with children to be reared, and an immeasurable weight of communal sin to be borne. But always amidst stern conditions has the glory of the Lord shone round about the sons of men. Moses was transfigured on a political errand to God, seeking the right sort of legislation by which to make a nation out of a tribe of degraded slaves. The ethical reality of Jesus' life was evolved by hard experiences. His moral glory was in the fact that it was an incarnation of, as well as in, the common life. While

Herod and Pilate govern the state, and wicked Caiaphas and prudent Nicodemus rule the church, with Gamaliel in the schools, the Messias comes a carpenter's son, bringing a peasant education, speaking the familiar accents of the common life, a simple man of the people.

The value of even that which is terribly personal, and which makes each profound experience in some sense exceptional, is finally its social value ; its redemptive value to the common life.　As was once said by Robert Louis Stevenson, himself one of the wholest and sweetest of human spirits, as well as one of the most helpful religious teachers, " We are all the inheritors of sin ; we must all bear and expiate a past which was not ours." We all feel ourselves deformed and beaten by the wilful or heedless irresponsibility of relations which are our responsibilities, and are all compelled to walk tortuous paths with bleeding feet because of obstacles and defeats pressed upon us by faithlessness. Some have one who utterly, and for all they can see hopelessly, prevents their life from being the moral glory it would, restraining it from its lawful career; one from whom they have a right to expect the gladdest and most living sympathy, and yet who lightly disregards all they hold sacred, ruthlessly outrages all their sacramental senses, and tears from their life the holiest expectations of youth and hope; one who hampers and baffles in such a way that they appear both to themselves and the world to be the wrongful rather than the wronged. But these are our social commissions; they are forces preparing our life for the social service, — the feeding of the sheep. Thorns in our flesh are our disgrace, and not God's glory, if they do not commission our life as a divine errantry among men, and become component elements of its social power. Our wrestling all night at Jabbok ford but morally weakens and emaciates, if we do not make restitution to our brother; to our brother of the tribe of Esau at that, and in clear violation of accepted economic ethics.

The divorce of piety from economics, with the consequent unmoral influence of religion and the degradation of politics, is indicated by nothing more clearly than the contemptuous meaning which has come to be attached to the word holiness. By the holy man is meant, in the popular thought, simply no man at all ; while the word primitively meant a whole human man, normally fulfilling all the natural functions of his life in their wholeness.   "The separation of the holy man from the virtuous man," says Amiel, is one of "the signs of a false religious conception," and "true Christianity must purge itself from so disastrous a mistake."   The Holy Ghost, or the Whole Spirit, is given to run the world with, and the teachings of Jesus are a revelation of the world rightly run.   The piety that finds market and state uninteresting as religious spheres, or that ignores them through material, intellectual, or spiritual interests, is a delusion and a curse. Devotion to God is complete sacrifice of self in the service of man, and ecstasies are without value that do not fruit in ethics.   Pure

religion and undefiled before our God and
Father is this, — to visit the fatherless and
widows in their affliction, and to keep un-
spotted one's self from the world. The clean
putting away of evil doings, the seeking justice and relieving the oppressed, is the condition upon which the Lord invites us to reason
with him in the things of religion.

Of religion as rightly related life, even the
early Puritan of New England, too much ac-
cused of the individualism which character-
izes his descendants, had a most solemn sense.
Economic pressure upon his religious reason
had much to do with his emigration. Writing
of England in 1629, John Winthrop says : " This
land grows weary of her inhabitants, so as man
who is most precious of all creatures is here
more vile and base than the earth we tread
upon, and of less price among us than a horse
or a sheep." " Children, servants, and neighbors," he writes, " especially if they be poor,
are counted the greatest burdens, which, if
things were right, would be the chiefest earthly
blessings." " Why then," he asks, "should we

stand here striving for places of habitation and in the meantime suffer a whole continent, as fruitful and convenient for the use of man, to lie waste without any improvement?" This he premises with the declaration that "the whole earth is the Lord's garden, and he hath given it to the sons of men." In the Confession adopted by the Puritan colonists at Salem on the 6th of August, 1628, they covenanted "to approve themselves to the Lord in their worldly callings, shunning idleness as the bane of any state, and not to deal hardly or oppressively with any." [1] Though he knew nothing of our social and economic terms, behind the Puritan's intense religious individualism lay a sublime social ideal. He would be free, but not with the freedom that was an end in itself; he sought freedom for the sake of what he conceived to be the godly brotherhood, the divine order. He sought a righteous commonwealth as the true manifestation of his religion. Sojourner that he was in a

[1] "The Pilgrim Fathers in New England," Dr. John Brown, pp. 287, 298.

strange land, refugee from religious oppression and political craft, he yet looked for a
heavenly country on earth, to be found in
holy political facts.

To-day, as a result of the material interests
that have absorbed both religion and life, we
scarcely have a religion ; we have no real
faith for which men are willing to risk life
and all. Churches and clergy, prayer-meetings
and benevolences, neither constitute religion
nor furnish social morality ; piety no longer
indicates righteousness, either in theory or
practice. Beloved brethren will wrestle the
night through, or at least a part of the night,
in revival prayers ; but the revival we need is
the restitution of stolen goods, of wealth
gained through oppression, extortion, and economic atheism. The rebuke of Edward III.
to the Pope at Avignon, to the effect that
" the successor of the apostles was set over
the Lord's sheep to feed and not to shear
them," is pertinent to our present religious
situation ; it is applicable to the priests of
the market and the popes of industry, who

are the now influential factors in organized religion. These will give feasts in the name of Jesus; but the testimony Jesus asks is the renunciation of economic plunder, and a sacrifice of self for the common good. Pastors may secure active participation in municipal reforms from the very men who buy the city's councils and loot its people, but only to find the city in a last state worse than the first. It is good that shepherds and bishops try experiments in the slums; but suppose they try the sacrifice of preaching the Sermon on the Mount from the pulpits of wealth! The church will accept philanthropies; but is it ready to be despised and rejected by the rich and powerful, that it may seek the justice of the kingdom of God?

Organized religion gives no sign of the great religious movement upon which the social salvation depends. Social faith and effort are moving on outside of, and largely in opposition to, organized religion; its leaders who come from, are not of, the church. As surely as Jesus found the Jews building up a religion apart from the human situation; as Rome was building apart from the human fact when Luther came; so we Protestants are now building apart from the human need that calls for our sacrifice. Dr. Parkhurst in New York is no more an answer to this charge than Savonarola in Florence is an answer to Protestant charges against Rome. Protestant Christianity, in that it represents property and religious systems more than righteousness and social faith, is practically a caste religion; and this in spite of its missions, exceptional institutional churches, and ludicrous willingness to receive the poor. With Dr. Bruce, I am a pessimist as regards the church, and an optimist as regards the kingdom. The hope of social democracy is itself the religious aspiration and effort of the common life to realize its sanctity; and organized religion offers no present channel for this realization. The church must repent of its manifest subjection to money, and free its institutions from servile dependence thereupon, if it is to avert the necessity of God's turning to the churchless peoples, or to the peoples regardless of the church, to find new channels for the redemptive life that is to heal the nations.

In fact, the influence of the church upon the social movement presents to me the greatest occasion of dread for the future. I confess this dread, with the fullest recognition of the anxious seeking for righteousness on the part of a greater number of individuals in the church than ever before. In a profound sense, the church affords to the forces making for social righteousness the unsafest possible leadership. Notwithstanding our persistent blinking of the fact, and our evasion of the moral responsibility it puts upon us, money has more influence than Jesus upon the ecclesiastical attitude toward the problem of economic equality and freedom. Any leadership the church would now put forward would be chiefly interested in keeping the social change bounded by the interests of mammon, and in preventing from accomplishing the actual social ideal of Jesus. It would thus practise a vast deceit upon the people, and the revolution of violence would then follow. In any safe social leadership of the church, money and houses, lands and railways, must bring on the moral agony of its preparation.

It is time, if the high time be not already past, that judgment begin at the house of God. If ever the religious needed to be told, in all the plainness of speech which the love of righteousness can conceive, that they cannot serve God and mammon, nor be both pious and covetous, and follow Christ while upholding an evil order, they need to be told this now. Like Jacob of old, we, the church, need to come to Jabbok ford, separating ourselves from the wealth that holds us in bondage all the harder that we feel it not, regarding no more our success in economic cheating and stealing as a mark of a specially favoring Providence, making restitution to the sons of Esau we have robbed, pursuing no longer a religion not the righteousness of God in human relations, that God may wrestle with us in all the power of the common interests of man, and then we may come forth a new church with a new name, with a moral glory that shall bring the worn and waiting multitudes rejoicing to our doors, to be led into the social Israel of organized love.

III.

THE LEADERSHIP OF SOCIAL FAITH.

1 Kings xix. 13–18.

DOUBTING Thomas and loving John,
Behind the others walking on : —

"Tell me now, John, dare you be
One of the minority?
To be lonely in your thought,
Never visited nor sought,
Shunned with secret shrug, to go
Thro' the world esteemed its foe;
To be singled out and hissed,
Pointed at as one unblessed,
Warred against in whispers faint,
Lest the children catch a taint;
To bear off your titles well, —
Heretic and infidel?
If you dare, come now with me,
Fearless, confident, and free.

"Thomas, do you dare to be
Of the great majority?
To be only, as the rest,
With heaven's common comforts blessed;
To accept in humble part
Truth that shines on every heart;
Never to be set on high,
Where the envious curses fly;
Never name or fame to find,
Still outstripped in soul and mind;
To be hid, unless to God,
As one grass-blade in the sod,
Underfoot with millions trod?
If you dare, come with us, be
Lost in love's great unity."

Edward Rowland Sill, in "Poems."

BERNARD never once seems conscious of his power, never appeals to his authority, never approaches to a command. He appeals to no sanction but their common faith; implores instead of threatens; bewails rather than rebukes. When he complains of a sin, he is the fellow-sufferer with the sinner; when he claims an act of justice, it is by appealing to the honour and duty of the wrongdoer. Whether he addresses pope, prince, or penitent, it is as one who is driven to implore, but who is utterly unworthy to command. Thus, from first to last, there is no trace of dictation, no consciousness of self, of any assumption of a right, no pride, anger, or rigour — there is nothing but the spontaneous outburst of a soul, which the sight of evil humiliates and hurts. — *Frederic Harrison*, in essay on "Bernard of Clairvaux," in "The Choice of Books."

III.

THE LEADERSHIP OF SOCIAL FAITH.

And, behold, there came a voice unto him, and said, What doest thou here, Elijah? And he said, I have been very jealous for the Lord, the God of hosts; for the children of Israel have forsaken thy covenant, thrown down thy altars, and slain thy prophets with the sword; and I, even I only, am left; and they seek my life, to take it away. And the Lord said unto him, Go, return on thy way to the wilderness of Damascus; and when thou comest, thou shalt anoint Hazael to be king over Syria; and Jehu the son of Nimshi shalt thou anoint to be king over Israel; and Elisha the son of Shaphat of Abel-meholah shalt thou anoint to be prophet in thy room. And it shall come to pass, that him that escapeth from the sword of Hazael shall Jehu slay; and him that escapeth from the sword of Jehu shall Elisha slay. Yet will I leave me seven thousand in Israel, all the knees which have not bowed unto Baal, and every mouth which hath not kissed him. — 1 KINGS xix. 13-18.

HISTORY records no braver faith than that of Elijah the prophet. Yet there came a time when Elijah despaired; when faith surrendered to disappointment, and the prophet would die with his work undone.

Through long years, in desert walks and

mountain haunts, he had brooded over the sins
of the people, preparing to work with God for
their reformation. To get the attention of the
nation, God had sent a famine upon the land.
Three years more the prophet had waited in
his hiding-place for the famine to do its work.
The time came at last to break his silence and
relieve the people's distress. "Go shew thy-
self unto Ahab," the Lord commanded, "and I
will send rain upon the earth." Elijah obeyed.
Surely now, he thought, the king and the kingdom would repent and turn to the living God.

The prophet arranged for a startling and
phenomenal display of the Lord's wrath against
the idolatry that had become both the state and
the popular religion. He gathered the apos-
tate people, with their false prophets, to Mount
Carmel. After the long exhibition of the impotence of the heathen priests, there came
the fire that consumed their altars. Under the
excitement of the great occasion the people
rose up and slew the false prophets, in obedience to Elijah's command. While they then
refreshed themselves with food and drink, the

reformer went to the top of the mount and prayed for rain. The rain came, and king with subjects hastened to shelter. Before the king's chariot, through the night and the storm, Elijah ran to the royal city of Jezreel, in the strength of the great hope that now wrought in his soul. He expected the reformation begun at Carmel to spread immediately through the whole kingdom ; Israel would now enthrone the worship of obedience to the living God as the religion of the nation.

But on arriving at the capital city, he was met with a message from Queen Jezebel, announcing that she had doomed him to the same fate he had brought upon the official prophets. The queen was the king's evil genius, whom the people feared more than the king. She was Elijah's bitterest foe, and virtue's worst enemy. If she was decided on the reformer's death, in the face of all that had taken place on Mount Carmel, after the awful day's work, with the bloody judgment upon the priests of the idolatry which the queen had herself largely introduced, then he must have lived and wrought for naught. If the forces of the state could be instantly turned against the living God, in the face of the commanding conclusion of the long, sad famine, then the national reformation was defeated at the outset. The hopes of the morning died away in a discouragement too great to bear. He fled into the wilderness, lay down under a juniper-tree, and slept in physical and nervous exhaustion, having requested of the Lord that he might die.

But in no such time and manner did the Lord intend to close the strong prophet's career. A messenger came and ministered food, in the strength of which, with the heat of his soul, Elijah travelled forty days and nights, coming to Mount Horeb, where he lodged in a cave. The word of the Lord came, inquiring why he was there, calling him to the strictest examination of himself, causing a purer knowledge and hold of the forces with which he had to work, and sending him back to finish the many things left for him yet to do. Bad as the nation was, its condition was not so hopeless as Elijah's despondency told him. There were yet seven thousand who would not bow the knee to Baal. Out of public view, peacefully following the plough in the valleys, quietly trimming their vines on the hillsides, perhaps ignorant of the crisis they were in the midst of, were men and the fathers of men who would keep alive the truth, through apostasy and corruption, to be borne on from generation to generation, deepening and widening in each, till the Messias should come and light the nations to God. Flowing in these humble and unnoticed servants of the Lord were streams of rich manly life-blood, yet to beat strong in the hearts of noble warriors, brave prophets, and great apostles. Elisha was there among them, unknowingly preparing his spirit to continue the work Elijah had begun, and link him with a long line of glorious prophets to come. Great potentialities of righteousness remained in Israel. The results of Elijah's labors were profounder than his provincial dreams, and to be finished vaster than the plan of his thought. His heroic faith was yet, through a disgraced and scattered people, to be fruitful in a righteousness that would become universal, making the nations of the world one kingdom of God.

The fact that there was more good in Israel than he saw was Elijah's call to fuller service, and not to silence and moral ease. Go back to your work, was the substance of the divine command. The unseen good was his obligation to be all the more industrious in preparing for the overthrow of the visible evil. He dare not despair because of the enormity of the nation's sins, nor yet form a selfish estimate of popular virtue that might excuse him from moral responsibility. Because of the seeming failure of his hard reform against intrenched and defiant wrong, he was not to spend his time henceforth exaggerating and flattering little goodnesses. He would have betrayed the hope which God had given him by being any less the virile and uncompromising man of effort than he had been before his disappointment. He had a right to hope only as he worked with God; and he could only work righteousness as he hoped with God.

Elijah's disturbance of the peace of Israel seemed just as unreasonable as the prophetic warnings of all ages seem to the people to whom they are immediately spoken. All things together considered, notwithstanding the famine, the kingdom was enjoying a high degree of material prosperity. King Ahab was not the mental weakling he is commonly supposed to be. Other strong men after him have been dominated to their ruin by the beauty and wilfulness of a woman. Ahab was a soldier and a statesman, with a forceful courage and a large grasp of affairs. He was a builder of cities, a promoter of commerce, and a successful diplomat. Under his reign the kingdom was prosperous at home, and respected abroad. What was all Elijah's fuss about? Simply this, that the people were mistaking certain forms of political and material aggrandizement for national progress, and had therefore become materialistic in their worship; it was logical that they should adopt a religion of physical forces.

Elijah's seeming failure, with his bitter disappointment, resulted from the individualism of his effort. He mistook unrealized potencies of the people for impotence, and did not apprehend the perfectness of the imperfect when used as social instruments. He stood alone, when he ought not to have stood alone; he should have known, and in some measure have organized, the possibilities for righteousness in the seven thousand faithful. He could work for man, but not with man; hence his work was rather for God than with God. He could not understand that divine opportunism by which God organizes all things, including evil, for righteousness. He did not know that when God cannot get what he wants he always takes what he can get. Elijah could die for righteousness' sake; but to live for right's sake in the midst of wrong, to be the divine incarnation and the living sacrifice, was more than he could bear. He could rise to the heroism of destroying wrong, but had not learned the vicariousness of healing wrong and converting it into right. He could understand the judgment of destruction, and of instantaneous and arbitrary setting up of right; but he did not yet understand the judgment of redemption. The lesson of Elijah's disappointment is that individual effort must be led by social faith; that faith in God will fail unless it be also a faith in the people. He seems somewhat to have learned the lesson, and to have put it into practice in anointing other chosen instruments to succeed him in his work; also in establishing his school of prophets, which school was not a theological seminary, but a centre of training for social agitation and political disturbance.

But the loneliness and mysticism that always mark the prophet are not strange when viewed in the light of his calling. The life that enters the fullest sacrifice of most fruitful service usually seems to the unseeing powers that be in its times, and to itself when nights of agony come on, to be either a foolish or wicked waste. Every prophet appears anachronistic to his age, which can see no sense in his being or speaking. He sees the march of nearing judgments, and by them interprets the meanings and issues of the movements in which the present is caught, while a great divine impulse he neither dares nor can suppress commands him to speak his truth to deaf ears, show his visions to blind eyes. There is the sound of swift approaching crises in his soul, and he grows weary with the weight of messages men heed but to misread. A nation's sins become his individual shame, the wrongs of the oppressed are his burden, and human destiny is alike his pain and joy. He is vicarious to lift his brothers by the power of his own ideals; knowing himself to be the brother of men in sin, he would make them his brothers in faith and effort. He is compelled to part ways with opinions he respects and characters he reveres ; with those whose fellowship he loves and whose kindnesses he has shared, in order to be true to the hope in him which seems hopelessness to the world. In keeping faith with himself, with the ideas and forces that commission and empower his life, he comes into square conflict with those the existing order calls its best, who are also highly satisfied with the world's opinion. Above all others he is bent upon the peace which justice alone can procure, and yet is regarded as the disturber of the peace of the righteous and orderly of his day. He is supremely an optimist, believing better things for his fellows than they dream of for themselves, and yet is set down as a brooding pessimist by those who contemplate the existing order with what a Scotch physician calls "that hideous foul easiness." An evangelist of mercy, he is known as a messenger of ill-omen and of wrath. He is sometimes wholly misunderstood by his friends, and most clearly understood by his enemies.

Nor can he wait for what our scientific conceit would call an exactness of statement. Napoleon III. is reputed to have once said that nothing lies like the truth; which saying is true. "Truth is as much greater than accuracy as poetry is greater than proof-reading," says Dr. John P. Coyle. There is an accuracy of statement which wholly belies the situation, while there is a divine exaggeration that is truer than the truth. The physician who would dwell on the healthy condition of a patient's hand, while the patient is just about dying from disease of the heart, is lying through the use of the truth. The politician who glorifies the deeds of the fathers, and accurately displays the great gains of the past generation, while the whole nation is diseased with political corruption, is a hypocrite and a traitor. The preacher who arouses himself and hearers with gains in church moneys and members, truthfully presenting certain facts of religious progress, with the increase of the righteous in the church, while the church in its institutional and authoritative attitude is at once blind and antagonistic to the cry and movement of the peoples for justice, is a false prophet and a liar. There are times when the most fatal falsehood is the utterance of what is strictly true. Jesus repeatedly and deliberately turned away those who were kindly and influentially disposed toward him, because of statements which, under the same circumstances, would seem to us untruthful and intolerable. The prophet cannot wait to put into order a system of social, political, and religious doctrine. He must leave many things true in themselves unsaid, because they would be untrue and delusive in the setting of the immediate crisis. Our notion that a man must present truth full rounded, so that right may be stated satisfactorily to wrong, and sacrifice presented agreeably to political and religious selfishness, would condemn and leave out of the realm of progress both Jesus and the apostles, with all the prophets both before and since their coming. What we conceive to be the full-rounded man has too often been of little use to progress, except to serve as ballast. No prophet has ever been reasonable or truthful to the judicious and representative minds of religion and state. The prophet's mission requires him to use the truth, not as an orb, but as a sword. He cannot blink the inevitable mortal antagonism of the vested interests of every sort in the existing order. Nor can he regard that chronic fright of originality so characteristic of mere religion, or that morbid nervousness of conservatism at every sign of growth. The preparers of the way of progress, the initiators of effort, are always men become the living incarnations of an idea ; they are voices crying the way. With such God makes straight the path for the coming of the righteous society. By the moral daring of such adventurers the kingdom of our God is pioneered. " There is no more sublime spectacle, — " says Victor Hugo, " mankind's deliverance from above ; the potentates put to flight by the dreamers ; the prophet crushing the hero ; the sweeping away of violence by thought."

But the prophet mode of progress is not the perfect mode ; and there is a better way of making history than the great man way. One human note is as ultimately necessary as another for the harmony of God's organ of humanity. There is coming a glad and tri-

umphant time when the kingdom will need no
voices crying its way ; though this does not
mean that no man will be exceptional or great,
but that all will be exceptional and great. The
unity of life in an unbroken harmony of progress that shall be nothing else than God in us
and we his people, the whole human life thus
becoming the Immanuel, is the end for which
God works and inspires.

> " For these things tend still upward, progress is
> The law of life, man is not Man as yet.
> Nor shall I deem his object served, his end
> Attained, his genuine strength put fairly forth,
> While only here and there a star dispels
> The darkness, here and there a towering mind
> O'erlooks its prostrate fellows : when the host
> Is out at once to the despair of night,
> When all mankind alike is perfected,
> Equal in full-blown powers — then, not till then,
> say, begins man's general infancy." [1]

The leadership of the faith of the people
is slowly but gloriously disclosing itself as the
better way of progress. It was something of
this that Elijah dimly saw and obeyed, after
Mount Carmel, the juniper-tree, and Horeb.

[1] " Paracelsus," Robert Browning.

This was distinctly the ideal of Jesus' kingdom of God. He that is least in the kingdom of heaven is greater than John the Baptist, though there be no greater personality born of women. Though none be so primarily necessary as the prophet, the least servant in the righteous society, the least apostle of its facts and forces, does a more constructive work. One thing greater than leadership is the greatness of being loyal to it, and of confessing it without shame, and with gladness.

Nor is the cataclysmal method of race development the substantial or final method. Though it has often taken generations of war and common suffering to teach man the fact, and give him the discipline, of a single idea, yet we shall not always need to learn through suffering ; not when we are able to learn otherwise. Not always will the noon glare of materially splendid civilizations blind the eyes of institutions and authorities to the judgments that are upon them ; the harvest sword of God will not swing in the human sky unseen save by the prophet. The unceasing change of

growth will not forever be an intensifying
strain and pain, while it ought to be an increasing harmony. The consummations of the
ages, the harvest judgments that are epochally
ending and creating anew the world, will yet
come and go without noise and woe. The temple of the righteous society will at last arise
without the sound of laborious toil, and with
the work that is the growth and melody of love.

The value of revolutions to progress has
been historically overestimated ; they have accomplished less in reality than is apparent.
I would not underestimate their social value,
nor question their historical necessity. But
they have put history backward as well as
forward ; they are always pulling up the wheat
along with the tares in their violence. The
Jewish revolt that came to an end under Titus,
though a revolt against oppression without
conscience or pity, is here significant. If the
nation had done as Jesus wanted it to do, at-
tending to social righteousness in itself, and
leaving Rome to plunder without resistance,
when the Roman fabric fell, because of its own

corruption and weakness, Jerusalem might have risen the actual rock and desire of the nations. Jesus must have brooded long and deep over the subject of revolutions. With the profoundest sympathy for the people whose wrongs drove them to revolt, his attitude against them, his estimate of their social failure, was profoundly philosophic. His doctrine of non-resistance was no pietism, but was the keenest and clearest apprehension of the law of social growth; he spoke not as a religionist, but as the profoundest social philosopher. If we knew how to let evil alone in the right way, it would come to an end. When we discover how to be opportune without compromising our ideals to the slightest shade, how to be expedient without being morally sceptic, we will cease to resist evil, and attend strictly to righteousness, with the final discovery that there is no evil to attend to, and that the thing we call the devil has ceased to be.

There is always more of good in the common life than appears on the social surface. While evil is assertive, and its organizations fall with cataclysmal noise, the good evolves from potentiality into the activity of conscious service more as the lily of the field. Revolutions at best but make way for evolution, as the thunderings and lightnings clear the atmosphere, while the rain and noiseless sunlight paint the beauty of the earth, and call forth its fruits. The confusion and violence must be met and subdued to order, but with the listening remembrance that the voice of the Lord is still and small, spoken in the faithfulness of the toiling thousands who serve without reference to Baal or mammon. Righteousness moves most quietly, while the kingdom comes with surest might and widest fulness. May not Frederick Froebel, the obscure and persecuted German teacher, by his kindergarten method and philosophy of education, ultimately have done more to make actual and permanent human history than any of the great military conquerors? While to our short and clouded vision the work of God seems slow, and we cry aloud for God to arise and shake terribly the earth, lest wicked men prevail, the spirit of right broods deep resolve in the common life and its prophets, creating unseen to us a new earth. When redemption seems hardly to prove itself a fact, and we mourn at the tombs of slain hopes, away beyond our faith the truth we thought ours is risen in the responsive faith of the peoples, leading them in gladness to liberty.

Much of the real and seeming evil of human life is moral ignorance, rather than deliberate disobedience. Countless human lives hunger for righteousness who know not where to find living pasture. Multitudes, both within and without the churches, are as sheep without shepherds, and yet are not only willing, but eager, to be led by shepherds righteous and fearless according to the ideal of Jesus. More feet than we can number, both of the rich and the poor, are scorched and bleeding in the search for some rock of truth on which to stand amidst the unrest and disorder. There is to-day enough of the social sense potential in human organism to render practicable the command that no one be anxious for the morrow. But civilization has so long been the power of the strong to exploit the weak, industry so long a war between the selfish for the spoil of the people's toil, organized religion so long the selfish appeal of institutionalism to the selfish interests of the soul, that the people know not yet how to rise into the liberty of the sons of God.

This moral ignorance is somewhere blamable; somewhere the ignorance of faithlessness to the social trust. John, the hostler of "Black Beauty," speaks sound wisdom about ignorance. "Only ignorance! only ignorance! how can you talk about only ignorance? Don't you know that it is the worst thing in the world, next to wickedness? — and which does the most mischief Heaven only knows." To this wisdom of the hostler ought to be added the wisdom of Jesus, that moral ignorance is wickedness. Farther back, might be taken the complaint of the prophet who was one of the formative influences of Jesus' life. Isaiah's burden, delivered to the priests and politicians of Jerusalem, was the moral ignorance they had wrought in the people. The people would not know and consider the right in distinction from wrong ; they refused to be ethically intelligent. Their ignorance of the right had come from the shepherds unconsciously growing into the mere hirelings of interests and parties. The tragedy of the human evolution has not been in the unwillingness of the common life to grow. God's trouble has never been with the peoples, if he could only find shepherds who would not become the hirelings of religious or political parties, of institutional or personal ambition to monopolize righteousness. The sins of the people are ever the fruitful result of the moral ignorance sown in the common life by the selfish design or neglect of faithless religious or political officials. Progress rises through the successive ridding of the people of merely official leaders, who prey upon the common strength and beat back the common freedom, and the raising up of leaders who are incarnations of the common life, its aspirations and efforts.

This is the chief social value of what we call great crises. As some crisis in the life of a man discloses nobilities in him that surprise his friends, and loyalties in his friends that surprise him, so a national crisis calls masterminded statesmen from among the people, with commanders of armies and prophet poets from the toiling ranks ; the nation suddenly finds itself rich in heroes of the common life. "There is," says Dr. Garth Wilkinson, the Scotch physician from whom I have already quoted, "a high law of order, of instant organization, which will inevitably range God's free men in his battalions, without preconcert, or coat cut to an external pattern."

The democracy of progress, calling for the profoundest social faith, is a fact of history writ large, but as yet read small. The high tides of the unceasing and increasing movement of righteousness bear into wide view leaders from the centres of power or sources of culture ; but these leaders have not been of the culture or power from whence they came. The spoiling of the Egyptians is an apt expression here. Moses and Paul, Luther and Mazzini, bring from the schools the spoils of learning, with the arts of power from power's centres ; but their real power and inspiration, with the actual education and forces of their life, come from the people. The literatures which the schools dissect and analyze, building up rival parties of learning, have been chiefly the creation of great moral passions and social efforts of the common life ; which passions in their rise were unknown by the schools, and which efforts were by them despised. The church always credits itself with the glory of the saints and prophets, with the efforts for righteousness they have led ; but that is after they have been stoned, outlawed, and slain by the church, and have risen from the dead, glorified in the triumphant faith of the people. Institutionalized power, political, religious, and scholastic, has been historic in its opposition to progress ; while the human value of mere scholarship is immeasurably overestimated, the social value of institutions greatly misunderstood. "It is the universities," says Henry D. Lloyd, "that are in need of culture, — of the culture of the workingmen in hardship, and equality, and sacrifice." Likewise, there is an immeasurable underestimation of the social value and creative power of the mere common feeling of the people after justice. The social faith of the peoples, the commonalty of their moral feeling, has been the power of God unto progress; while the powers that be, and the students, are busy here and there, doing the works of their imaginations, believing not the word of God in the people, although the true end of institutions is to hear and execute this word.

The whole movement of the Protestant Reformation had in each nation a certain ground of social hope in the common people, which has been obscured by succeeding theological controversies. The Reformation of Wyckliffe was largely an effort of the English people for the justice they could not get from feudal lords so long as they were supported by the priesthood.[1] The Lollards were mainly persecuted and put to death for reasons that were not at all theological, or even religious in the current sense of that word, but for causes that were distinctly economic; they were animated by a passion for social justice, and were known as the anarchists and destroyers of political order in their day. The Reformation in France seized Calvin by the force of its need, providentially compelling him to be its champion, and had in it the hope of political freedom. Luther was the articulation, rather than the cause, of the German Reformation, which had its rise and strength in the German peasantry.

Jesus based his claim to Jewish recognition on the fact that he was a development of the people. He was always trying to show his organic relation to the national and social evolution and to the universal preparation. He

---

[1] "History of the English People," John Richard Green, vol. ii., chap. iii.

was the flower of the fulness of his times ; not brought forth as some magical or supernatural being, but as the perfect work and glory of the common forces at work in human life. Dr. Edwin Hatch calls studious attention to the great revival of morals, the wide and deep effort toward righteousness, issuing from the Stoics, which had prepared the Græco-Roman for Jesus' coming.[1] It is as unfair in church historians to point to the Roman and the Greek cities as a true picture of the best that pagan religion could do for the people, as it would be for a Buddhist to point to the slums of London and New York as the natural fruit of Jesus' teaching. Whether we are conscious of the cause or not, it is because their common life found in him at his coming, and has increasingly found in him since, its personal incarnation and objective revelation, that the people pray to the Father in the terms of Jesus. Man prays in Jesus' name because Jesus is the expression of man's conscious

---

[1] " The Influence of Greek Ideas and Usages upon the Christian Church," Lecture VI.

manhood, as yet but potential and unrealized. The people believe in Jesus because Jesus believed in the people. Human life will commit itself finally to this Son of God because he is the Son of man, bone of our bone, flesh of our flesh, the glory and ascension of our common effort. God became the incarnation of man in Jesus, as well as man the incarnation of God; God always has to become man before he can work and rise with man. The social revelation of the incarnation of God in the Son of man, and in history, is the immediately pertinent lesson of this the social hour.

To-day society is under deep conviction of sin, conscious of a corruption which mere reform cannot heal, sensible of a guilt which neither revolution nor legislation can bear away. Society is also asking what it shall do to be saved, day by day convinced that it has as yet no organized power by which to accomplish the social salvation. But who, or what, shall deliver society from its weight of sin and guilt; from the strain and distress that baffle the wisest and make the bravest doubtful;

from the social shame that overwhelms, and the social ruin that impends?

The times are prolific of social solvents. Many of the programmes proposed for the evolution of social knowledge and order from the present ignorance and confusion are good, so far as they comprehend the problem of society. All of them, even the wildest social schemes proposed, are potential with the elements of the power that will yet unify all elements and forces in a social regeneration. But not even the best programmes satisfy our various interests, commercial, scientific, and theological.

We are asking for men who will outline for us the new social system; for a science which shall detail for us the full particulars of a new social organization. We wait for some one to offer us a complete programme of social reform, and point out to us each step in the fulfilment of the programme, before we proceed to right our social wrongs, or believe in the nearness of a juster society. We would know by what paths we are to move, before we set out toward a better civilization, before we commit ourselves to a social ideal. We imagine we are willing to walk by sight; but we are certain that the safety of society depends upon our treating as offenders any who would have us walk by faith. As a bright friend of mine says, "First move the ship, then steer;" but we are exhausting ourselves in trying to steer social progress without moving it; that is, to make progress that shall not be change.

But if we are to learn the future of society, and work with the social forces that are to prevail, we must learn from the feeling of the common life, which has more to give us than we to give it, and must become its living incarnations. From all sorts of respectability, good Lord, deliver us, may have to be added to the prayer of progress. The universal social crisis we face calls those of us who would work with these forces to the fullest apprehension of the leadership of social faith. The common life is eager and adventurous as never before with the messianic forces that are to make the righteous society. President Eliot has a touching expres-

sion about "the uninformed public opinion of
the west." As a matter of reality, the somewhat undeformed common opinion of the west,
notwithstanding all that may seem wild and
vague, is a surer social prophecy than any
voice that the university has yet raised. The
social talk in the rude mining town, in the
railway-construction camp, on the mortgaged
farms of the Dakotas, will afford a clearer
view of the social future of our nation than
can be seen from the point occupied by economic or social science. The authority of
human life is spoken even in the angry demand of the mob for justice, and the triumphant persistence of moral forces can be
heard in the rude appeal of the demagogue
and the agitator. The glory of God is shining everywhere in the social expectancy and
earnestness of human faces. The better civilization will be wrought at last by the social
feeling of the people, by their natural and
untutored sense of divine justice, without regard to those of us seeking a science of society, and very likely in ignorance of our having

existed. The social feeling of the common life is always a more intelligent and commanding guide than all the wisdom of political and social philosophers. The voice of the people is in truth the voice of God, and the feeling of the people the pulse of progress. The chief value of what we may get from the schools, from the most accurate social sciences, from the most careful facts that expert observers may gather, is the art they may give us to interpret the voice of God in the people. Whatever the simple feeling for justice in the common life says ought to be is the authoritative word of what will be, notwithstanding the conservatism of our interesting sciences and vested interests. This word must be our teacher, if we are to be scientific in any true sense, or are to stand before men as reformers who speak with the authority of the living God.

Some of us cry unto God to send us men like unto the old prophet reformers of the Hebrews. But that God spake to the Hebrew people at certain times, in a certain

manner, is no sign that God will ever again
speak in like manner to other nations. History never repeats itself. God needs no more
Elijahs or Jeremiahs. God wants not prophets, nor the sons of prophets, but men, — divinely human men, — moving in the normal
order and common experiences of human relations ; men without ill balances, or even
what Carlyle would call righteous eccentrici-
ties. It is not the spirit of Elijah or John
the Baptist that shall now go before the
face of the Lord to prepare the way of his
coming in a new order of things, but a
more whole and human spirit. The Hebrew spirit has done its work, — a good
work, but, historically, a finished work, not
to be done again. We also cry for a new
Luther, a Savonarola ; we would call into resurrection the spent spirit of the Protestant
Reformation, the Puritan Revolution, or the
early spirit of the American movement for
the abolition of slavery. But the spirits of
these have done their work, and not their
work is needed now. A Luther would be a

calamity, a Savonarola an added burden, to the forces at work in the social regeneration. The spirit that gave national salvation and Cromwell to England would now put history backward. The spirit that abolished slavery would not be able to bring forth order from amidst present social conditions. The reformers of history have all done the work of God in their way and time; they have been divinely chosen men, and have followed divinely chosen methods. But God neither wants, nor will there be, a social reformation, but something deeper, more enduring and diviner. The reformer might be animated by the loftiest enthusiasm that reformation can inspire, but not be able to prepare the social way of the Lord, whatever good he might accomplish, however great his achievements and triumphs.

They who look for the coming of the holy society will be compelled to choose between the way of Jesus and the way of any of the reformers who have given their life for the world. From the way of reformers the way of Jesus radically diverges. In the most fundamental sense, we cannot be a follower or disciple of any reformer or patriot and at the same time a follower and disciple of the Lord Christ. They who prepare the way of the new social kingdom will be quickening spirits, rather than political or religious reformers; and through them the regeneration of society will proceed without observation, while the politically and religiously wise are mocking their impracticability. Though antagonized beyond all others, they will not be antagonists, but witnesses of the divine order that is slowly manifesting itself in the world-consciousness, and that has always been the foundation of the world's progress. They will be lights before whom the social darkness will retreat, almost without men's discerning that the darkness is passing. And when the Christ order of human relations appears, men will wonder by what means it has come.

By the social faith of the people we shall have to move out of the old and into the new order at last. No new social system will be accurately outlined, no programme completed, by which we may advance with the successive steps in view. Society will not be saved by statistics, and will not act according to the fictions of abstract economics. The new civilization will not be the creation of the merely intellectual forces at work upon a science of social origins, phenomena, and diseases. Nor will it be made by political hammer and saw. It will be the political outgrowth of a religious evolution of the common life. Its foundations are descending silently out of heaven from God; and its masonry will rise without noise amidst the social confusion and possible violence, — the work of unseen hands, the creation of spiritual forces.

The leadership of social faith requires of us the fullest and most generous recognition of the values of each other's works and words; requires that we seek to accredit all our progresses to the common life, keeping ourselves as individuals, and our systems of thought as well, out of sight. Not only must Elijah discover the good in the existing or-

der, and be willing to work with his brothers
from Elisha to Jehu, but the good in the existing order must respond to the good in
Elijah. If the best conservatism in existing
institutions would consider its need of Elijah's singleness of vision, its need of that
ideal of absolute right he cannot yield though
it slay him, and would not suffer the powers
that be to outlaw him as a vagabond, or
threaten to sever his head from his body,
Elijah might not so often despair in over-
whelming conviction that conditions are even
worse than he has seen. We are alike prone
to judge of the value of each other's work
by its immediate effect upon our own, judge
of the value of each other's words by their
bearing on our present plans. We each
apply narrow, selfish, and individualistic meas-
urements to the worth of each other's efforts for the righteous society. If another
man works in a way that crosses our own
work, or that seems to deny our cherished
convictions, we therefore decide the man to
be inexpedient or dangerous, when it may be

we are each sounding distinct notes of the spirit that socializes and saves. Our unwillingness to suffer men to cast out devils in any other way than ours, or to cast out the particular devils we feel ourselves better fitted to cast out, is in itself a sure sign of our own social unfitness. When we who would prepare the way of his kingdom have faith enough in God to trust each other, to believe in the religious value of conceptions that appear to contradict what we have learned and taught, to rejoice in the social value of efforts that seem to cross our own, to be not so fearful for the course of righteousness outside ancient channels, then we will hear our teachings that now seem widely at variance becoming accordant notes of one psalm of progress, and human life will see in our efforts that now seem divergent a glowing prophecy of the blessed relations of the nearing heavenly society.

IV.

REPENTANCE UNTO SERVICE.

John xxi. 17.

It frequently happens that repentant sinners become more holy and pleasing to God than those who have never fallen. There are a multitude of persons who go through life in a safe, uninteresting mediocrity. They have never been exposed to temptation; they are not troubled with violent passions; they have nothing to try them; they have never attempted great things for the glory of God; they have never been thrown upon the world; they live at home in the bosom of their families or in quiet situations; and in a certain sense they are innocent and upright. They have not profaned their baptismal robe in any remarkable way; they have done nothing to frighten their conscience; they have ever lived under a sense of religion, and done their immediate duties respectably. And, when their life is closed, people cannot help speaking well of them, as harmless, decent, correct persons, whom it is impossible to blame, impossible not to regret. Yet, after all, how different their lives from that described as a Christian's life in St. Paul's Epistles! I do not mean different in regard to persecutions, wanderings, heroic efforts, and all that is striking and what is called romantic in the apostle's history; but (if I must condense all I mean in one word) in regard to unselfishness. All the peculiarity of a Christian consists in his preferring God and his neighbor to self, — in self-denial for the sake of God and his brethren. — *John Henry Newman*, in "Sermons on Subjects of the Day."

I HAVE lost everything and lost myself; and yet, O God, Thou hast kept my life's desire alive within me. Thou hast not blotted out before me the aim which has caused my sorrows, as Thou dost before so many thousands who ruin their own lives, but Thou hast preserved my work in spite of my errors. I was drawing near to my tomb in hopelessness, but Thou hast filled my evening with brightness, and softened the sorrows of my life. I am not worthy, Lord, of Thy compassion and trust. Thou alone hast had pity on the crushed worm; Thou hast not broken the bruised reed, nor quenched the smoking flax, nor hast Thou ever averted thy face from the offering which, from my childhood, I have striven, but striven in vain, to bring to the outcasts of the world. — *Henry Pestalozzi*, in a written prayer.

126

IV.

REPENTANCE UNTO SERVICE.

He saith unto him the third time, Simon, son of John, lovest thou me? Peter was grieved because he said unto him the third time, Lovest thou me? And he said unto him, Lord, thou knowest all things; thou knowest that I love thee. Jesus saith unto him, Feed my sheep. — JOHN xxi. 17.

THE rally of a strong man's faith, after the moral shock of his unexpected fall into some deep sin, is the mightiest effort of God in a human life. By the power of such an effort Peter took his place as leader among the apostles, after he had denied his Lord, proved himself falser than his eleven brethren, and brought upon himself something of the shame of Judas.

Peter had not meant to sin; his was no deliberate falsehood, or thought-out abandonment of a course of life. But a man does not need to be a cool and calculative sinner to lose his moral balance in the moment of crisis; even to have fair become foul, and foul become fair.

Strong passions know no moral mathematics, and are controlled only by affections and faiths stronger than themselves. Through long years some holy dream of a man's soul may be so selfishly cherished that, when suddenly facing either possible realization or probable defeat, it becomes a passion without thought or will, drawing the man's whole being into its concluding and uncaring leap. Then reason becomes unreason; while the hand of God seems to slacken the reins, and the soul discerns not between the flames that lure to death and the lights that shine for life. It was somewhat so with Peter.

It is with the strongest gentleness that Jesus meets the impetuous and repentant apostle; the gentleness which spares no humbling of pride, no restoring pain, that it may render Peter plastic for the divine mould. You have fallen, Peter, at the point where you thought yourself safest of all. You boasted of your greater faith, of a devotion which could not be tempted; yet these your brethren have been truer than you. You were blindly obeying

your self-will, when you thought yourself **my**
closest follower. What think you of yourself
now, Peter? Lovest thou me more than these?
Peter this time makes no assertion of greater
devotion, nor hints at any comparison of personal values. He does not even use Jesus'
word for the highest quality of personal and
religious affection, but a word of weaker meaning, as a literal translation shows. Not only is
the spirit of self-valuing gone, the shame of
his failure will not let him confess the love he
knows to be in his heart. He turns back the
appeal to the divine appellant : Lord, you know
whether I love you or not ; you know that I
am at least fond of you ; look into my heart
and see. But yet more must Peter be humbled, and that in the presence of his brethren.
Thrice had he denied his Lord ; thrice must
he anew confess him. The third time Jesus
accepts the apostle's own word, and makes no
reference to the other apostles. Are you sure,
Peter, that you are even fond of me? Then
Peter was grieved at his Lord's moral probing
and seeming persistence of distrust. But he

makes no claims for himself. He simply casts himself into the arms of that unsparing mercy, that all-knowing love. Lord, my destiny is in your hands ; to you I commit myself for judgment and command ; you know all things ; you know that I am fond of you ; I have learned the lesson of my failure ; surely you do not believe I will fail again.

Then, if your failure has freed you from the weakness and tyranny of self-will, and you now love me above yourself, realize your repentance in service ; vindicate your apostleship in sacrifice for the kingdom I have revealed and initiated. Feed my lambs, Peter ; strengthen my weak ones ; shepherd my sheep. When you were young you felt yourself strong, and you were self-reliant. You were borne about upon the impulses of your self-will. But it will be so with you no more. I have saved you from yourself ; and from the depths into which your passion of self-will plunged you, my spirit has lifted you up. Henceforth you are mine, Peter, redeemed by the sacrifice of service, to which your life is henceforth committed. You are no more at your own disposal. The currents of redemptive providence will bear you in unseen ways you would not have chosen. And when you are old, others will bind you and lead you to death, as I have been led. You have nothing more to do with your destiny, save to accept its glory of sacrifice. Your times and seasons, your words and works, are appointed you of my Father, whom I have made known to you; in his way I will lead you from now on. Idle no time in looking back; waste no strength in faithless remorse; nor fear the future. Through our fellowship of suffering and triumph in redeeming human life, I will make your failure and shame glorify both me as your Redeemer and you as my redeemed one. The denial of self in behalf of your brothers, your continuous sacrifice upon the altar of human need, can alone vindicate your devotion, remit your sin, and make your broken career whole, with your repentance sure and glorious.

Thus the first value of Peter's repentance, after his restoration, would be its value to others as a redemptive force. As the woman of Eden is promised salvation through the bearing of children, so Peter is promised an effectual repentance through the moral birth he shall give to other life than his own. He who, being the leader of the apostolic fellowship, had sinned most deeply and repented most sorrowfully, would be the one to understand most sympathetically the dangers and needs of the sheep. The greatness of his sin would give him a sense of oneness with the weakest and worst of his brethren. His own failure would make him slow to condemn, and quick to serve. The farther he advanced from his sin, the more frightful it would appear in the clearer light of purer years, and the stronger would be the gratitude compelling him to the Redeemer's service. The tradition of his rising every morning at the same hour at which he denied his Lord, and going alone to pray anew for forgiveness, whether true or not, is expressive of the heart and career of the apostle's after life. We are not surprised to find him the most passionate proclaimer of the need and fact of redemption. It was fitting that through great sufferings and daring adventures of faith, by brave deeds and fruitful words, and at last by most painful martyrdom, Peter should prove his devotion, and glorify the apostolic brotherhood.

Peter's character being what it was, his disgrace was essential to his development and equipment. Not until terrible catastrophe had annihilated his selfish faith, and he had thus been brought very low, was he able to do his divinely appointed work in the divine way. God does not order evil that good may come, but he so organizes evil tendencies as to bring them to an end. The apostle's failure was the revelation, and therefore the judgment and cure, of the evil persisting in his previous career. The fall of the man was also the fall of his sin. Being tried at his strongest, he found self a failure. Where he thought he of all others was safest, he fell the lowest, save one. Before this fall he had been pursuing the phantom of life, which is power for one's self; now he laid hold of the reality, which is the service of one's brothers. He had been a man of extremely generous impulses and very selfish principles, ready to serve in an individualistic way, but impatient of co-operation with his brothers in mutualism of effort. His unsocial individualism had led to his fall, and he reached repentance through a social process. The social realization of individual repentance is thus the distinct lesson of Peter's restoration to his apostleship and brotherhood.

In the leadership of the past the personal repentance of certain strong characters has been the most effective social force of religion. This is the characteristic of Hebrew and Christian religion. The Hebrew genius and aspiration have the one idea of redemption; and the gospel of Christ and the kingdom is the revelation and message of redemption accomplished. Moses, David, and Isaiah are lifelong penitents, the consciousness of specific sins seeming to effect their most redemptive deeds for the Hebrew people, and to be the organ of their most comprehensive visions of human perfection. From Paul to Augustine, from Luther to Finney, the sense of personal sin to be expiated, or of sin forgiven, often making for deformity as well as righteousness, has impelled the most strenuous religious effort and service. The quickening messages of judgment and redemption have been best preached by men quick with the consciousness of having been redeemed. The great world-helpers have somehow, sometime, known themselves as great sinners, moving through the flame of the pit, coming forth maimed for life, with right arms or right eyes consumed away. Upon his most responsible errands God has sent men forever humbled by sin, made memorable by thorns of bitter regret ; men purified by suffering that would consume body or brain should they neglect to work out their salvation in vicarious service.

Of course, the profoundest processes by

which the greatest human values are made do not appear. All that is deepest and holiest in the bravest and mightiest lives, all that is best and costliest, is felt but not seen. Their life is hid with Christ in God — hid both from themselves and the world. The world feels the power of the divinely possessed and offered life; the machinery of the world is safer because of the life's presence; but the world sees not the secret springs of its power. The world thrives on the worth and rejoices in the strength of strong, white souls; but the mighty forces that move them, the deathless loves that inthrall them, the divine visions that lead them, — all are hid from the world's eyes. The hopes of men are lifted by the revelation of some new truth; but the school in which the prophet learned the truth he speaks is hid away in the hills of God. The soul of the world rises upon the inspiration of great poetry; but it reckons little that the genius of poetry is also the genius of suffering. The courage of the world leaps with the wine of an intensely consecrated life ; but it sees not the wine-press of anguish in which the feet of God have trodden out the wine. The world feels a new security in the presence and power of one who is manifestly a man of God ; but it catches only faint flashes of the hid fires that are consuming the dross. Thus the master influences that mould the thought and history of the race are largely invisible.

Even while we rejoice in our world redemption by the sinless and therefore greatest sufferer, we know little of what Calvary meant ; the deep darkness of Gethsemane no eye but the Father's has ever pierced ; the weight of the human woe that crushed out the cleansing blood of the Lamb, none but the infinite love knows.

Could all these world-helpers, like the One, have come forth unblemished from the wilderness of experience between innocence and virtue, that would have been good ; for that is our human destiny. But it is infinitely better to be tempted and fall, and then be redeemed and equipped for service, than never to have been morally proved and made. The redemptive value of untried innocence is simply that of the raindrop and the apple-blossom. It is the goodness achieved through tremendous moral processes which counts in the service that redeems. The old Peter was a crude and worthless man compared with Peter refined and restored. One hour of a redeemed life is worth more for God's human service than countless ages of a merely innocent life. The kingdom of heaven is not to come through the pleasant studies of intellectual butterflies of culture, or the delightful exhortations of religious connoisseurs, but by men to whom sin and redemption are the profoundest facts of knowledge and experience. The smallest fragment of a man saved from mortal conflicts, purified in the heat of moral convulsions, has a social worth which Adam could not have possessed by living in unproved innocence until now. No man is good for God's redemptive service, good for much in any sphere of human development, until he has met and triumphantly fought the battalions of wicked devices which the powers of darkness marshal before the advance of every chosen soul — and every soul is chosen. Only give God a man, and he will pay any cost, or take any risk. A universe of material worlds is but as a grain of sand when valued with the man who images God's idea of human life.

Then the fearful failure of life is not in having sinned, but in never having given one's self to a positive righteousness, with its enthusiasm for moral conquest. Not the blameless life, the faultless conduct, makes up the great human thing to be desired, but the passion for the increase of right. The career which customary religion and social judgment see to be worthy, and even spotless and exemplary, is often at best a mere negative, a moral cipher. Not the having done no wrong, but the having done right, is the end of living morality ; and right doing is always some form of social sacrifice.

Remarkable enough to our religious valua-
tions, Jesus never condemned sinners as such ;
he condemned only those who did not know
themselves as sinners. This attitude he expressed in the keen irony of the statement
that he came not to call the righteous but
sinners to repentance. His burning and un-
qualified denunciations were for what the Jews
took, and for what we take, to be the blameless life, the faultless career ; for those who
thought themselves more righteous than
others, and therefore more meritorious of
providential benefits. The difference he saw
between men was not that some were sinners
while others were not, but that some saw only
their brothers as sinners, while others, with
their individual sin, felt the moral pain and
shame of all human life as a guilt and suffering of their own, to be personally expiated.
Those who have the truest individual conviction of sin have the greatest social sense of
sin ; they feel their share and guilt in the sin
of the world, and take it all as their own to
bear away. Instead of losing their life in

seeking an individual extrication, they find their life through losing it in the universal extrication. It is thus that God has been obliged to make some of his greatest saints out of greatest sinners. With only such as know themselves as sinners, see themselves to be yet undone and unmade, has God been able to work out our one human moral creation. The truly repentant awaken to the largest social conscience, though they may not know what has come to them, and may express themselves in the most individualistic terms. Repentance is a social process and a social realization.

Now, as the redeemed life grows into the redemptive, its course becomes more and more that of the true penitent. All increase in faith, in devotion to our Lord's service of man, is an increase in genuine humility. We come to see, even when we place our whole life upon the altar of human need, how little there is we can render unto our Redeemer in return for his redemption of our life. The deepest and largest life, and the richest possession and costliest sacrifice, are cheap and inadequate

when we measure them by the cross of our
salvation. It is not meet, we sometimes feel,
that Christ's holy name be on our lips. The
more intolerant we are of sin, the deeper and
uglier the sins we find to root out of our
hearts. We are paralyzed more by our own
follies and failures than by the sins and mis-
judgments of the world. What we thought
to be love for Christ and the pursuit of his
righteousness for man, often proves to be an
insidious self-love. We do the greatest harm
where we meant to be most helpful, and work
death where we meant to give life. We see
in ourselves, in moments of moral candor, the
evil things we most abominate in others. In
those hours of rare spiritual honesty, when we
look at ourselves in God's mirror of the Christ,
and there behold the ethical realities of our
life, we confess to ourselves that we have no
strength to war against the hosts of selfish
impulses, the pride, the frivolity, the envy, the
lust, the self-deceit, the hardness and exclusiveness, by which we seem overthrown. And
when we think of arraying our own weakness

and folly against the powerful and honored wrongs of the world, it often seems that we can do no better thing for man than get out of God's way, and leave his work to purer faiths and stronger hearts than ours.

But there are individual experiences of judgment and repentance, the issues of which infinitely outweigh the daily penitential experience. An unexpected crisis comes which finds a man in what appears to be the last ditch, fallen there and helpless to rise. As with Peter, the fall in itself is not the thing of consequence, but the long course of self-will and false values it discloses and judges. Upon the power of the man to rise from that extremity of weakness, with its utter exhaustion of moral nerve, God seems to stake all his interest in not only the man himself, but in his redemptive utility and world mission. What looks like the last. effort of a divine desperation to save, before the soul's case is finally closed, forces upon human helplessness the supreme struggle which mightiest human strength would pale to meet. All the forces of the universe are felt to be straining for the life or death of the man, in the revealing moment of choice and destiny.

Nor is the moment of revelation and destiny always brief as to time; it may stretch into years. We sometimes long pursue a course of life we think righteous, suddenly to awaken to the fact that it is wrong and deadly, while we seem unable to find a way into the right. There come days of blackness, when we would know the truth about ourselves at any cost, and yet we know not whether we be God's or Satan's. The lake of fire would be gladsome, the worst torment an ecstasy, if it would only burn up all self-deceit and hypocrisy, all self-will and faithlessness, and show us our ethical realities; while the most imagined bliss of a material heaven would be an intolerable horror, if it disclosed not to us the naked truth about our life. There comes an hour, so great is our moral agony, in which we care not whether there be a God, if only there be a sure right in distinction from the surely wrong. But, having sometime held back from the promised land of moral freedom, we are doomed to wander in the wilderness of bitter perplexity. Are the angels of light we follow sweet and holy messengers of duty, or disguised demons of delusion and ruin? Is the path we walk a way of unrecognized self-will, or the way of the Lord into the service and wholeness of sacrifice? Are the words we speak for truth the voice of one crying the approach of God in a freer human life, or the alarm of a diseased human spirit? Is our agony the gnawing of the worm that dieth not, or is it the simple want of an adventuring faith in the way God would take our steps? These are not strange questions, if our religious experiences have touched their heights and depths; if we are witnesses and reporters of the actual processes of our spiritual evolution; if we have introduced the scientific method into the subjective world, so that we are able to speak words of life we have touched, tasted, or handled; if we have gone through the wilderness of ethical perplexity into the realm and motivity of moral freedom. I do not say that these have been the needful facts of our ethical progress, or that man will continue without end in this wilderness; but they are the actual facts we meet in the subjective world, which is after all the real world.

But whether the revealing moment be long with moral scepticism, or quick with vision and instant with decision, it wakes us to moral realities by a matchless agony, in which we face two immediate ultimates. One of these means loss of faith in the existence of right, with disorder and ruin of soul and mind, the death of the body coming last, — spiritual, intellectual, and physical disintegration. The other means the rise of faith to moral vision, regenerating the spirit by a wholly new perspective of human relations and resources; enlightening the reason with the beginnings of an endless knowing; renewing the body through commanding it to wait on the Lord in his service. As Epictetus has said, ours " is a storm, the greatest of all storms, the storm of strong suggestions that sweep reason away." "The contest," he says, "is great, the task is divine; it is for kingship, for freedom." Knowing ourselves caught in the mighty movement of forces that will grind us to powder, or else recast our life in a new mould yet hid from us in the thought of God, we can only pray to become plastic in the hand that unmakes but to remake, until we are made perfect.

Repentance unto service is the end for which God risks us in these judgment processes, involving our utter ruin a while, or else our birth into a wholly new world of moral consciousness. That righteousness may increase and abound, are we thus afflicted with revelations of our sin. For a social fruitage too great for our thought, and a destiny too wondrous for our faith, the love of God chastens us by experiences so profound as to hide their full meaning, even after long years of suffering and service. If we come forth from these processes fully repentant, our minds turned from self-seeking to feeding the sheep, though we bear a life-long shame into our service and a thorn in our flesh, we can glory in our weakness because of the strength it will be to the brethren, and rejoice even in the gnawing of the worm that dieth not and the fire that is not quenched. The soul that has squarely met and conquered the forces of conflicts so mortal, whether in the pit or on the heights, has felt what Paul calls the birth pangs of the labor of God for the divine sonship of our creation. It has literally changed its attitude toward God and human life, turning from the unconscious pursuit of individual happiness to the conscious and deliberate pursuit of service as the sole rightness of life and the one common human good. It will bring forth fruit worthy of repentance, fit for the social food and gladness.

An enduring repentance is always a social realization; it is a change of mind and life from the service of self to the service of others. Not by inward brooding, in mere subjective processes, can repentance fulfil itself; it must be worked out in service, and save itself by moral adventure. Upon the merciful errands of the kingdom of God, in the corners and by-ways of hid and helpless need, on the open field of moral conquest, along the highway of social crusade and sacrifice, by brave redemptive deeds and fruitful saving words, must repentance prove its reality and vindicate its confession. Repentance that is not an immediate and continuous turning to service, and that does not become a grateful social mission and a gracious moral chivalry, soon ceases to have truth and value; and then its form and profession become the hypocrisy of life and the curse of religion. It is the social feeling that produces repentance; and through the rise of this feeling in unselfish interests, and its growth into generous actions, does repentance remake and glorify life.

There is no holier and more beautiful example of this than the much misinterpreted story of the thief on the cross. He was probably not a thief, in the usual sense of that term, but a member of some guerilla band of revolutionists, and evidently a very noble man by nature. The " dying thief " knew nothing of the salvation we talk about, but felt that some significant and tremendous wrong was being done that marvellous patient man on the other cross, and his heart made offer of all he could give. Only after he had exhausted his possibility to help, did he make the simple human request for a kindly place in the memory of him whom some called Lord, when he should come in the better justice of the kingdom which every Jew was, rightly or wrongly, expecting to see realized in his nation. Through the medium of sympathy that turned his mind from his own suffering and disgrace to the defence of his sacred fellow-victim, the robber was unknowingly touched by the glory of the great sacrifice taking place beside him. It was his instinctive and thoughtful concern for the suffering and public injury of another, his honest and chivalric human feeling, that gave him such instant fellowship

with Jesus, and made the grateful fellowship thus begun upon these two crosses of
torture, each supporting its dying victim as
a decreed outlaw, a veritable paradise of God,
a communion of heaven, on the earth.

Repentance unto service is nothing else than
the simple acceptance of the salvation which
Jesus sacrificed himself to procure. To repent
is to turn one's mind from self-seeking to the
service of others, and to accept the sacrifice of
self in order to serve as the law of one's life.
Jesus meant his life to illustrate this law so
fully and powerfully that at last all human life
would repent by turning to it in willing and
loving obedience, and the kingdoms of the
world thus become the kingdom of God. He
did not come to protect us from God, but to
deliver us unto God, and protect us from ourselves. He did not come to make God different from what he had always been, and always
will be, but to show us what God eternally
is, that we might be propitiated and made
satisfied with God's kind of life, and receive
the law of his being and working as the law of

our being and working. His sacrifice was not a substitute for righteousness; it is the eternal definition of righteousness. Jesus' righteousness saves no man unless he has it; it does no man good beyond his practice of it in his life. There is no righteousness but the sacrifice of love in service. Jesus' sacrifice thus shows us what we are to repent from and repent to, so that our repentance may be intelligent and effectual.

Then no man realizes the repentance by which Jesus saves until he offers his whole life to God upon the altar of human need. Jesus' sacrifice saves one, or makes him right, no more than it repeats itself in his life. We are not reconciled to God through Christ until we are reconciled to the life that exhausts its possibilities in the sacrifice of service. By accepting his sacrifice as the law by which we live do we accept Jesus as the Christ, and become Christian in fact. To follow this Christ means to follow him where he goes, into the midst of the world's wrong to set it right. He who tries to follow Christ only for what he can get out of him is not saved, but lost; he is not truly repentant, and may be the worst of self-seekers. Judas is the one example of a man who followed Jesus simply for the sake of what Jesus might do for him.

It is with repentance that the greatest moral dangers come, because of the religious ignorance of its social necessity. The selfishness from which Jesus came delivering, theology has made fundamental to the gospel of deliverance. It has changed the ground of moral appeal from the kingdom of God to an arbitrary system of selfish rewards and punishments. The salvation of giving one's life to the good of God in others has been changed into a sterile religious self-interest. The call of Jesus to deny self, and renounce all that one has, in the service of bearing away the sins of the world, has been perverted into a call to accept a scheme of individual escape to some other and unreal world. The appeal of Jesus to life, to the divinest human ideals of holiest sacrifice, has been set forth as an appeal to death, subverting the gospel of the kingdom, and denying the reality of redemption.

The doctrine of divine punishment, as it has been preached, unremedial and unloving when not penal or vengeful, has been at once a false gospel and a destroyer of effectual repentance. Punishment itself is a revelation of life, and it is to life that punishment appeals. The very sin of men is a revelation of their sonship in God. The misery of men, when they drink the dregs of sin, marks the difference between what they are and what they ought to be. The ruins of men attest their moral dignity as sons of God. The wickedness of men is the measure of their capacity for goodness. It is the fact of what it might have been, and may yet be, that makes a life wasted in self-seeking so awful a spectacle, so solemn a tragedy.

Then not to death, but to life, with its service and destiny, is the appeal for repentance to be made. All the forces of God's universe make for life, and not for death. The world is redeemed, and sin has no more dominion over us. Unto us have been granted

all things that pertain to godliness. We have
a right to hearts untroubled and unafraid.
In the world we have tribulation; but the
Son of man has overcome the world, and redemption is the fundamental reality. Sin
abounds; but grace much more abounds.
The billows still roll over us; but there shall
be no more sea. The night is dark a while,
and we see not yet as we are seen; but there
shall be no more night. Death is swift and
triumphant now, and the hunger of the grave
insatiable; but God shall wipe away every
tear, and there shall be no more death. Devils rage, plot, and destroy; but hell shall be
cast with death into the burning lake.

This carries no comfort to the sinner who
wills to sin, as some would have us mean,
but only terrible warnings of immeasurable
woe. Since "we live indeed in the kingdoms of redemption," as Rothe says, "and
no more in the kingdoms of this world," we
have no excuse for acting as though we were
not redeemed; no excuse for obeying the
laws and maxims of selfishness. We cannot

get away from the kingdom of redemption, nor the pursuit of its forces, except by moving out of the universe; and there is no other to move into. We have no choice but to accept this redemptive economy and its facts, with its laws of sacrifice by which we are redeemed, and the moral destiny which Jesus its initiator reveals. We may be sure that only deadly consequences can follow the moral scepticism that ignores this redemption and denies its law; be sure that we shall have to be reconciled to our destiny at last, though it takes æons of the flames that increase our sufferings with their fury as life hardens. If there were some place where a man could get away from God and his kingdom of redemption, from its unchanging facts and pursuing forces, to be abandoned to the utter and inconceivable isolation of undisputed self-will, there might be a sort of comfort in even that depthless, matchless misery, that fabled condition of the lost. But whither shall we flee from his presence, and whence can a man get beyond the scourge of the love of God? If we ride the winds of the morning to the uttermost parts of the earth, or find a way to reach the most distant stars, the wrath of the Lamb will be there with its judgments. If we make our bed in the grave, we cannot make sure our soul will see corruption, even when it would. The love of God is in the foundations of hell, to light its fires; we can go there only to be with God, and face our destiny anew and more terribly. The disordered reason will still be haunted with meanings struck forth from the law of Calvary, which is the sole law of the universe, having dominion over the whole and each minutest part, whether the parts will or no. The universe has no smallest secret place where the vision and law of Calvary can be escaped. "We live indeed in the kingdoms of redemption;" and we can find nothing else to reckon with than the facts and forces of its universal economy.

Modern Christianity, with all its works of power and words of truth, has never felt the force of the apostolic conception of redemption.   Even the Hebrew prophets had a far larger thought of redemption than theological Christendom.   They suffered and wrought in the vision of a redeemed world and a perfected human society.   The Scriptures are possessed with the idea of redemption as a social reality.   It is human life and all its activities, not a number of individuals, that its prophet and apostle writers conceive to be redeemed.

Of course, this kingdom of redemption seems hardly to prove itself a reality at times.   We see the hardest and most Christless ethical scepticism domineering as strictest religion, while much the world calls doubt is but the cry of the divine childhood of men unto the Father of their life.   Loveless spiritual pride, atheistic piety, religious unbelief in rightness, —the things our Lord rebuked with such unrestrained scorn and consuming anger, — sit in judgment upon souls that travail in the moral anguish of a vicarious service.   Great religious assemblies distract the church and nation with strifes of words about definitions, while wickedly ignorant and silent as to the social crimes and legal robberies of the churchly. Organized misrepresentations of Christ appear before the world as defenders of his faith and protectors of his truth.

Then the great doers and witnesses, the faithful servants of the race, have not seen in the flesh the results of their faithfulness. Those who have worked hardest to right the wrongs of the earth have gone to death amidst apparent defeat, disaster, and disappointment. Elijah and the prophets, Paul and the apostles, Savonarola and the reformers, Mazzini and many other witnesses to the Christ in human life, went to their rest in the cloud of immediate failure.

Yet the most glowing prophecies of universal righteousness have been born in the throes of sacrificial suffering. The rejected Isaiah saw the whole earth at rest, brotherhood between men and nations accomplished, the fields and forces of nature obeying man's moral law, and a political righteousness realized that was able to effect social peace and quietness. It was Jesus' vision of the cross of his own agony that widened to take in the human world : "And I, if I be lifted up from the earth, will draw all men unto myself." John saw the new heavens and the new earth from his prison rocks on Patmos. While waiting in Rome for the executioner's sword, Paul wrote his letter of heavenly consolation to the Philippians, promising that every knee in heaven, on earth, and under the earth, should yet bow to confess Jesus Christ as Lord, to the glory of God the Father. The restored Peter, sent to realize his repentance and glorify his shame in feeding the sheep, and to succeed his Lord and the Baptist as the messenger of repentance to his nation, foresaw "the times of restoration of all things, whereof God spake by the mouth of his holy prophets which have been since the world began."

Thus the great faith in God's good ways and times, the eager expectancy that all wrong is being made right, inheres in the holy passions that are able to cause that sacrifice of life which bears away the sin of the world. A man's faith in human life comes to be measured at last by his self-denial in human service. They believe most in the redemption of the world who are engaged in actually redeeming it; who commit themselves most fully to the service of their brethren; who turn their minds wholly to feeding the sheep. We have the largest and most commanding visions of a redeemed and righteous society when exhausting our possibilities in social sacrifice. The human redemption will prove as real to us as our repentance, and the human prospect as divine and glorious as our service. Wherever there is a rich and fruitful life pouring itself into the world, there is a soul uplifted and uplifting with a hope for man which failure only deepens and widens.

So every moral step of the individual, every rise from a fall and renewal of effort, is so much social strength and gladness for the world, so much service and power given into the hand that remakes and makes perfect.

The work will be no failure; however long it takes, soever sore the making and remaking process, it will be finished in righteousness. For Christ himself is God's eternal judgment on man; and to be like him is our destiny, while to serve like him is our repentance.

V.

MATERIAL WORLD AND SOCIAL SPIRIT.

ROM. VIII. 20, 21.

AND thus at length we see what human progress means. It means throwing off the brute inheritance, — gradually throwing it off through ages of struggle that are by and by to make struggle needless. Man is slowly passing from a primitive social state in which he was little better than a brute, toward an ultimate social state in which his character shall have become so transformed that nothing of the brute can be detected in it. The ape and the tiger in human nature will become extinct. Theology has had much to say about original sin. This original sin is neither more nor less than the brute inheritance which every man carries with him, and the process of evolution is an advance toward true salvation. Fresh value is thus added to human life. The modern prophet, employing the methods of science, may again proclaim that the kingdom of heaven is at hand. Work ye, therefore, early and late, to prepare its coming. — *John Fiske*, in " The Destiny of Man."

I HAVE heard it asked by cynical young men, who imagine that religion is at an end because they have none themselves: But why should I live for others? Where is this law of love in nature? Where, one may ask, is it not? Nor could a question more completely illustrate the anarchy of thought which is at the bottom of many of our " present discontents." The conception of self-sacrifice is, of course, no invention of Christ, or any one teacher; it is the inevitable outcome of social existence. It commenced long ago, when barbaric man first realized that, if he and his fellows were to live together in any comfort, it could only be on some basis of give and take. To live absolutely each man for himself could not be possible if all were to live together. In course of time, in addition to utility, certain more sensitive individuals began to see a charm, a beauty, in this consideration for others. Gradually a sort of sanctity attached to it, and Nature had once more illustrated her mysterious method of evolving from rough and even savage necessities her lovely shapes and her tender dreams. To assert, then, with some recent critics of Christianity, that that law of brotherly love which is its central teaching is impracticable of application to the needs of society, is simply to deny the very first law by which society exists. — *Richard Le Gallienne*, in "The Religion of a Literary Man."

164

V.

MATERIAL WORLD AND SOCIAL SPIRIT.

For the creation was subjected to vanity, not of its own will, but by reason of him who subjected it, in hope that the creation itself also shall be delivered from the bondage of corruption into the liberty of the glory of the children of God. — ROM. viii. 20, 21.

PAUL could not tolerate a fragmentary conception of life. He must have a cosmic philosophy, a philosophy of history that would also be a philosophy of life, in order to keep his sanity, and work with intelligence and increasing hope. The demands of his intellect needed to be satisfied, in order to keep him from living in a chronic state of moral inflammation.

The apostle's letter to the Roman Christians is his philosophy of both nature and history. That which we know as the eighth chapter is the greatest word on evolution that has been spoken, with the possible exception of some expressions of the prophet Isaiah.

The dependence of material forces on human character, with the social nature of that dependence, is a true expression of Paul's idea in what we have divided into the twentieth and twenty-first verses of the eighth chapter of the Roman letter. To the end that the sons of God might be evolved from its processes, the whole creation was subjected to vanity, not of its own will, but according to the reason of God. But our English word vanity is an inadequate and now misleading translation. Literally translated, Paul says that the creation was subjected to transitory nature, to things that change and pass away. This subjection was strictly an ethical process, with a glorious deliverance in view. When man should at last awake to his full and destined relations with God, to his ethical relations with the forces of nature, and thus realize the universal priesthood of his life, the natural forces from which he had been evolved, whose subject creature he had been, would in turn become subject to him, obeying his righteous will. The material world, in all its operations and manifestations, would become man's obedient servant, the responsive instrument of his thought and moral touch. This was the liberty of the glory of the sons of God, upon which God had set the hope of his heart, and upon which the eager outlook of creation was fixed.

In this, Paul was characteristically Hebrew. The Hebrew mind was never able to conceive of natural forces as other than forces of righteousness. The sympathy between the morals of man and the actions of the physical world was fundamental to Hebrew thought. The unity of life which is the ground of the newer philosophy, the sociality of all life and forces which evolutionary science has discovered, was assumed as a matter of course in Hebrew political and religious thinking.

By no other than this evolution from natural subjection to moral sovereignty can the full freedom of man be realized. Man is not free until he has made subject his subjection to the physical, and entered into the freedom of God to use the material as the language of the spiritual; until there are no more happenings in human life, man is still struggling with his brute inheritance. The liberty of the glory of the sons of God is an ethical liberty; it is the liberty of right living. Freedom is not the capacity to choose between right and wrong. Men do not sin because they are free moral beings; they are not free moral beings because they sin. No man is born free, neither Adam nor Jesus; no man is free until he has made intelligent and loving choice of the right. Freedom is right relations; it is the realization of the power to command through obedience.

Subjection to transitory things, to processes of evolution and education, did not necessitate sin. We cannot put upon the natural facts and forces in which our life is rooted, and by which it must grow, the responsibility for sin. Nothing is evil in itself, and sin is not in the nature of any sort of things.

It is the abuse or disuse of a thing, making it a negation of God and his righteousness so that it counts for nothing in growing the moral man, that makes it sin. Things become evil by our using them for other ends than God's great human thought. When Paul speaks of the mind of flesh, he does not mean that flesh is evil, but the fleshly mind — the mind absorbed in providing for the comfort and convenience of the flesh. The mind of flesh is sin and death because it has fallen into the service of the flesh, instead of using the flesh in that moral service which ever rises toward the freedom of perfectness. Life falls by turning inward upon self and downward upon the flesh; it rises through turning outward in service and upward in spirit, obeying the will that shall at last subject all physical forces to a finished moral and social creation.

God did not mean we should sin, but he could prevent our sinning; sin is in the world because God could not, without our conscious working together with him to that end, keep it out. God has and ethically uses all the power there is, and this subjection was the best he could do for his creation; he could do no more and act morally. Speaking after the manner of men, there was no way by which God could create human life without taking the divine chance that it would move through sin in its evolution, education, and perfection. So God made the eternal venture, in the hope that even through sin man would yet come forth in the freedom of a perfect creation.

God thus cannot make man free save through man's conscious and willing co-operation, God and man becoming of one mind, and working the same works. God is a social being; his reign is a social reign. The Father of men would not be even their accepted moral tyrant. He will rule with, not over, man. Liberty of sonship is conscious co-operation with God; it is the power to use the power that God uses, and for the same ends.

If all this means that we must give up

the philosophic absolute God, why not? We shall have no great loss, and the gain of a Christian God and universe to our thinking. Better than thinking, we shall come to hold with God a human and social fellowship, having found him to be a Father, with feelings like the children who are his offspring. For no philosophic, passionless peace is God's. The conception of a God without passion is at one time Buddhistic and at another pantheistic; again Roman, and then Calvinistic; at last materialistic. But the God whose fatherhood Jesus revealed is love; and love is passionate, or it is not love. The unending regenerations that make the progress of man, the divinities and vitalities of his nature, are the passions of God. The unresting activities with which the universe lives and grows are the energies of God's affections. The truths of men are flashes from the soul of God, the heroisms and reformations of man God's enthusiasms.

The social dependence of every sort of life upon every other sort accounts for human experience, and becomes the ground of our common hope. For slavery or freedom, we are bound up together, and with us the beneficence or destructiveness of the physical elements. It is not numberless unrelated individuals, either separated or aggregated, but our whole human life, with the woof and warp of physical creation in which life is caught, that jointly travails in birth-throes for the sons of God. If there yet remained one life out of relations among men, and every other life were living by faith in the righteousness which God has defined by the sacrifice of his Son, human life and its physical world would still be disordered, sorrowful with redemptive pains. It is this creative and redemptive agony of toil, in which God and all human life jointly travail together with our material world, which prophecy and science are alike seeing in various ways, that now appeals to the individual to consider the whole sacrifice of life as but a reasonable service.

Man's relation to the physical world is thus

wholly an ethical relation; it is also a redemptive relation. The material universe is not mere matter, consisting of chemical affinities; it is a living and spiritual thing, sympathetic and suffering with the redemption and destiny of man, dependent upon his social spirit. Without the ethical co-operation of man with God, nature itself cannot put forth its fuller glory, or disclose its hid treasures of goodness and beauty. The perfect order and good of the physical world are dependent upon the moral order of the human world. The prophet was truly scientific in saying that the wilderness would blossom as the rose, and the deserts become watered gardens of the Lord, when the redemption of man from sin into wholeness should be accomplished. Thus conceived, the physical earth becomes the object of sacred care and affectional interest, and the stones beneath our feet cry out to the sons of men to manifest themselves as sons of God. The winds are thus God's messengers, with the lightnings his social revelations, and the mirage of the desert his command to social service, while the air we breathe is the living breath of his infinite soul. Edison and Nicola Tesla are thus preparing the way of the Lord, as truly as Luther and Cromwell. The material becomes spiritual, and the spiritual divinely material; so that we have a new materiality with a new spirituality. This spirituality of the material suggests the need of a new term to denote the idea of the unity of all the elements of life, both conscious and unconscious, to the common understanding.

Spiritual and natural harmony are one and the same thing. Who knows but there would at last be no accidents, and the forces of nature have no furies to destroy, with men in perfect harmony with God? Behind the destructive effects of nature, there seems to lie the destructive self-will of man. We are having revelations of this in many sorts of recent investigations. Scientific men are beginning to tell us that desolating wars of past centuries are one cause of the earth's cyclones, its droughts and deserts. It is not only that climate makes the man, but also true that man makes climate. Mazzini notes that Athens and Sparta had the same climate, but that one produced man's greatest intellectual development, where the other failed, because of the difference in character between their respective institutions. While individual greed and social infidelity bring physical perils through the waste of our American forests, the new social conscience undertakes the irrigation of arid lands. The author of "Three Months in a Workshop," that delightful social narrative that comes to us from Germany, in giving a certain instance, says: "So a small technical invention becomes a great social and ethical influence — in this instance for good — and accomplishes more than many sermons and other efforts at reforms." Even in the realm of the artificial, we have had the President of the United States seeking to awaken legislative interest in the fact that the thousands incidentally slaughtered in railway traffic need not die, if the national sense of the sacredness of human life were equal to the national sense of the material values of corporate gains.

The sciences, with social investigations, are thus unconsciously, and as if by divine accident, viewing human life from the point long ago reached by Moses and Isaiah, Jesus and Paul; and they are reaching it faster by far than the church, which has the oracles of God's seeing ones committed to its care. The physical sciences, which we once thought leading us straight to atheistic materialism, are now unknowingly working with the prophets and apostles of Jesus to lift human life into a higher and vaster realm of motivity.

In this realm we meet with Jesus, discovering that no statement of the natural law and fruits of man's relation to the physical world has ever been so exactly scientific as his words spoken to the multitudes on the mountain. Warning them to lay up the treasures of life rather than the treasures of material gain, he shows so simply that this heavenly treasure of life consists in the social service; that only by each man living for the social righteousness, can the productive and distributive processes of nature become the organized bounty of God, supplying each according to his needs, while each according to his powers engages in the social service. According to Jesus, what we call the accumulation of wealth is not only not natural law, but is the improvident distraction of nature, as well as a frightful social disease. Social democracy, with economic equality, thus becomes at once the realization of both natural law and the religion of Jesus.

Material dependence on spiritual relations makes credible and rational many things which pass the belief of thoughtful men, and which have never been accredited by them save through a sort of blind faith. The influence of mind over matter has come to be the unwritten creed among skilful physicians of even the most conservative type ; and it is the creed of their practice much more than of their theory. One of the most honorable and professionally trusted practitioners of the older school of physicians recently said to me, that many such as he could no longer place a limit on the psychical or spiritual influences upon the health and life of the body ; that the chief effort of the advanced men of his profession now is, first to get the patient into right relations with environment, and then as fast as possible into a harmonious state of mind. Notwithstanding all the follies and irrational practices that result from wrong conceptions of the fact, it is none the less coming to be a fact of consciousness that disease somehow springs from sin and ignorance. Sickness is false or unsocial relations. The knowledge and practice of health promises to be one of the revelations and gains of the social pursuit of righteousness. John Inglesant is made to tell how, with swaying and clouded reason, he kept from insanity by walking for two years with his mind steadily fixed on God. The holiness of God in human life is the perfect moral, mental, and physical wholeness of man. Disease will sometime be treated through moral diagnosis.

The ethical or social nature of health simpli-

fies the whole matter of Jesus' miracles. I
have no opinions to offer as to the actual oc-
currence of all the miracles he is said to have
wrought. My faith has so little to do with
these, that I can almost say that I am indiffer-
ent as to their historicity. Yet they present
scarcely any difficulty to either my reason or
my faith. Being the perfect ethical being that
he was, the one whole Son of man, it was
wholly natural that Jesus should work what
we call miracles. In reality, there was nothing
supernatural about them, or about anything
else, so far as Jesus was concerned. Standing
in the relations he did, in harmony alike with
God and the material universe, it was natural
that physical things and forces should obey his
will. Disease could not exist in the harmony
of his presence. It was natural that he should
reveal love as the healing and regenerative law
of nature ; natural that the Son of man in perfect harmony with God should command the
natural forces and elements, and that the winds
and the waves should obey him. Instead of
being an exhibition of something supernatural,

the miracles of Jesus simply reveal man in ethical relations with nature, and nature in normal relations with man. They reveal the waiting social harmony of all life in the fully manifested sons of God.

It is in its social forces that the immortality of life inheres. By the immortal we usually mean that which is everlasting; but everlastingness is simply the incident of immortality. We are not immortal because we exist. It is moral strength, not existence, that is immortal; moral strength, not existence, that outlives death. The immortality of life is not some vague individual bliss — the meaningless existence of pietism; it is the persistence of moral or social forces in personality. The individual life may be said to be as immortal as the ideal in which it is invested. The social nature of righteousness once understood, immortality becomes easy of understanding; indeed, almost anything else becomes inconceivable. Progress furnishes many historical instances of the power of a great idea to take up a frail body and give it, if not health, a virility and capacity to endure that exhaust and astonish the strong. I think I can understand a little of how the passional force and momentum of a great idea could pick up the physical Jesus from the tomb, and send him about his work. With his life caught in a world movement that was to go on unto the world's perfection, death became impossible, even ridiculous. Jesus could not die, any more than righteousness could die. Why should I die? If my life is all invested in working the works of Jesus, in accentuating his idea and realizing his ideal, what have I to do with death, or death with me? Suppose I to-day experience what men call dying, I cannot see that it has anything to do with my keeping on with the work to which my life is committed.

Individual immortality depends upon the social spirit of the individual, on the strength and reality of his love, on the vitality of his relation to the social organism. It is, as it ought to be, the race life that is immortal; and the individual becomes immortal through fulfilling his life as a function of the race life.

With the immortality of the race life we are all the time face to face. We see that life does not die; that the life of each generation is borne on to the next, to be increased and still borne on. It may be that we shall one day see that only the lack of unity, our trying to live as fragments or dismembered members, keeps us from whipping death from our midst. Perhaps it is as a man of divine vision that Mr. Howells speaks, in one of his novels, when he suggests that the mystery of death will be taken away when the law of love prevails on the earth. Humanity at its worst, through all its unexplained sorrows, along the darkest labyrinths of its pilgrimage of progress, has never been without some spirits pure enough to see a deathless and perfected world. Sin has never been deep enough to rid the race of an inner consciousness, a consciousness it yet fears to hear or articulate, that death is an intruder and enemy in the world, having no place in a normal and perfect order, and that when sin is eliminated the factor of death will disappear. However that may be,

it is upon the redemption and socialization of
the common life that the immortality of the
individual must found its hope. This has
been so perfectly said by Jesus, in speaking
of his person as the living centre of the
human organism. "I am the vine," he says,
"ye are the branches: he that abideth in me,
and I in him, the same beareth much fruit:
for apart from me ye can do nothing. If a
man abide not in me, he is cast forth as
a branch, and is withered; and they gather
them, and cast them into the fire, and they
are burned. If ye abide in me, and my words
abide in you, ask whatsoever ye will, and it
shall be done unto you." Acting together as
members of one living organism, nothing is
impossible to men, while a glory the eye hath
not seen nor the mind conceived awaits them.
But acting as independent and unrelated individuals, and not as the living members of the
one organism of their human life, they become fragments, to wither and be burned in
the fires that consume, purify, and remake.
And they who abide in the human organism

as living members will never be lonesome, though left alone, for all the tides of life that flow from God through man will fill them with his joy. Upon the fundamental assumption of the universal sociality of life Jesus bases his religious conceptions, builds his social ideal, and grounds his promises of immortality.

The material or social interdependence of all sorts of life is the chief fact to be considered by progress as a whole, and by each individual life. In the yet struggling childhood of man, as well as in the fuller growth to come, there is nothing to be gained but by our standing together. We can never realize the truth of our life by individualism, by independent action. The mystery of life can never be known by each seeking to solve the problem for himself. The kingdom of heaven, so I have somewhere read or heard, is not an anarchy of good individuals. No man can be, or ought to be, wholly saved until human life is saved; and it is impossible for any soul to be saved or lost alone.

Without us, Abraham and Moses, Elijah and Paul, with all the prophets and apostles since, neither can nor would be made perfect. The perfection of the individual can be completed only through the perfection of the human whole.

The social basis of life commissions love as the sole guide to the highest knowledge. Our rude sciences, so given to analysis that disintegrates rather than empowers, have separated man into absurd departments, dividing reason from faith, the affections from the intellect, facts from feelings, work from passion, love from knowledge. But we shall one day learn that these are only the childish and ethnic beginnings of the science of man. Our scientific superstitions will sometime give place to the truer science of man as a whole, as a microcosm. Then love will no more be divided from knowledge, but will become the power by which we know, mighty to save and build. The things which eye hath not seen, nor ear heard, and which have not entered into the heart of man, are things of life, hav-

ing to do with life's organization and perfection, and are treasured in the store of God
for them that love. The great forces of
the universe, which are ours to be received
alike through spirit and nature, cannot be ap-
prehended for the vaster and wholler organization of our life, save as they are sought by
the social love. Only the adventure of love,
in search for social treasure, can discover the
unknown physical properties and spiritual resources of our life; these are ours with which
to build the holy city, when love shall teach
us how to use them.

> " We must never part.
> Are we not halves of one dissevered world,
> Whom this strange chance unites once more ? Part ? Never !
> Till thou, the lover, know; and I, the knower,
> Love — until both are saved." [1]

The redemption and perfection of the human
organism requires of its members the fullest
possible participation in all the relations and
experiences of life. Jesus came, not destroying human life, but saving it through the re-

[1] " Paracelsus," Robert Browning.

demption and sanctification of its relations. The Christ-life opposes all that savors of asceticism and moral cowardice, religious aggrandizement and social secularism, regarding each of these as a worst atheism; for atheism is the absence of God, or the denial of righteousness, in human relations, — it has nothing to do with religious opinion. The gnostic lies that have so long cursed philosophic and religious thought, darkening the mind of Christendom as an evil shadow, and paganizing its ethics, atheizing its industry and politics, should have no more dominion over us. Our human nature is not inherently evil, not dualistic and divided, as these lies have taught us, but is one social and holy life coming from God. Not to frighten us out of the world, or to make us pious atheists in the world, but to make every human relation a religion, with every human intercourse a social sacrament, was the ideal of Jesus. There is a wicked correctness of conduct, a lawless reverence for authority, an immoral chastity, an atheistic piety; and the worst of these, because the parent of them all, is the atheistic piety that is the substance of official religion, and is the logical desire of the plunderer and the oppressor, the hypocrite and the ecclesiastic, in all nations. To withdraw from responsible relations and vital experiences with every phase and force of society, for reasons material or religious, intellectual or merely individual, and to seek religious development as something other than the righteousness of love in these experiences and relations, is to try to sanctify fatal selfishness, and make practical atheism holy. Every individual is a social problem; and the whole problem of society is every individual's responsibility, his call to the most comprehensive social service and the richest possible social experience. Each individual soul is a universal problem, and the destiny of the whole universe inheres in each individual soul. There is nothing actual or potential in human life that is not substantially an indispensable element in every individual's ultimate development; and without this development of every individual, neither he nor the human organism can be made perfect to survive the strain of the eternal becoming of the universe. The problem of society is the problem of the whole human life, in its seen and unseen spheres, in its known and unknown forces, in its universal and individual relations; and the destiny of no individual can be separated from the human whole. With the social interdependence of all life must each individual career first of all reckon, and upon this ground must every social structure build, from it every social aspiration rise.

Even what we call individual self-consciousness is really a consciousness of relations; there could be no individuality except as a function of the social organism. The full realization of human individuality is through universal sociality. Each individual life is a universal function; the whole universe is man's social sphere. Albeit the highest, man is but one mode or incarnation of the universal life.

By only an intolerable morality then can

happiness be said to be the lawful pursuit of the individual life. While we idly say that theories have little to do with practical life, the man who is at this moment bargaining across the counter, the man who has just manipulated the rise or fall of certain stocks the man who has just decided upon what street he will build his house, the preacher who has just decided what set of doctrines it will be safest and easiest for him to hold, is simply acting out a theory of life formulated long ago by the philosophers. The assumption of happiness as the pursuit of the individual life, as the reason for political liberty, and as the ground of religious appeal, is the acceptance of a false theory that has borne much of our social wrong as its evil fruit. The pursuit of happiness as the end of life is the fundamental social error and vice; it is the social anarchy out of which we are struggling. The doctrine is the persistence of a pagan and anti-social ethic through Christian forms and phrases. It is the deliverance of life to the servitude of transitory

things, and from the liberty of the glory of
the sons of God ; thus precisely reversing
the order of nature which Paul presents,
making life a devolution rather than an
evolution. In other words, the pursuit of
happiness, which is the founding of life on
its happenings rather than its realities, is
life's complete enslavement and degradation.
It is also a real worship of material things
and forces, far profounder than anything con-
templated at the heart of the primitive nature
worships. From the delusion and misery,
the tyranny and cruelty, of the pursuit of
happiness, we are making it hard for the
good Lord to deliver us. No fate can be
more fearful than one of happiness in a
world like ours — a world of sin and expiation, of birth-agony and death-mystery, of
social sacrifice, calling every life and power
and affection to its altar. To be willing to
be extricated from the common pain and
social shame, from the storm and stress of
faith and social travail, is to desire the happiness of the dead whom Jesus would leave to

bury the dead. The pursuit of the social righteousness, with the whole life made sacred as a sacrifice thereto, is the only reasonable pursuit of life. One's work can be lawfully decided upon only with reference to its fitness for enabling the individual to carry on his social pursuit. The individual is a living instrument by which God may procure the common good; his life a function by which God may feed the social organism with universal life. By no tolerable ethic can the individual pursue other than the ways and means of making his life the fullest possible sacrifice to the common life, while taking from it the least possible for the supply of his individual needs.

Nor can this pursuit of happiness masquerade in the sophistry of an enlightened self-interest as the law of life. We should begin to learn from Jesus and nature that he that saves his life loses it; that even a social service performed for one's own sake is immoral in its individual aim and effect, whatever its value to society. Not self-interest,

but the social interest, is the natural law of
the individual life. Interest in one's self, in
one's own happiness, as the law of life and its
pursuit, is the cheat and fraud of life. The
only interest in one's self ethically conceivable
is an interest in making one's life the best possible social function; in making one's self the
best possible social member to be fitly joined
to the social body. But by no honest definition can this be called self-interest. It is
really the highest interest in the social well-
being, and is the truest form of self-sacrifice.

The individual life is then a social quest, a
search for social treasure, an adventure in the
holy society. Our sacred pilgrimage is alike a
way of sorrow and a way of glory, making life
an unending discovery and exploration ; a continuing trial and experience. It is true that
we walk by faith and not by sight ; that we
must betimes endure to find the right of yesterday, for which we would have died, to-day
so wrong that to abide in it is death ; that
what we shall be does not yet appear. But we
know the way we take. It leads into the fully

realized freedom of our eternal sonship, into the moral glory of a social transfiguration such as no white passion of ours can conceive, upon which perfect goal the eager outlook of creation is fixed, for which gain God and his universe ardently wait. Although we are still in the making, and are not yet manifested in the image conceived for us in the heart of God, yet every human instinct prophetic, every human potency that glows with moral vision, promises our perfection in the messianic ideal of the holy society, and commands each life as a sacred function for its realization. While our universe is an eternal becoming, opening an infinite prospect of adventure in knowledge and love, yet human life is not an endless development, never to be satisfied or fulfilled. Evolution has its limits; God's things get made, and his works finished. The works of God are not slow for the perfectness in view, while the world is yet very young, its animal instincts still clinging hard, and its social infancy scarce born. The matchless cathedral I have seen was built through centuries of war

and change, of violence and desecration, of lost
and restored plans; yet steadily climbing the
light, it stands there finished at last, a dream
of God wrought into stone by his divine men.
If we will be at peace with God's work, re-
sponding obediently to his whole way with
each, taking each our place in the living temple
of the ascending humanity, through all storm
and stress our work will abide, with our life a
glory of God. Deny we each the self that
would betray our life's search, estrange life's
social quest, missend life's holy adventure;
then ours will be the joy of continuous de-
crease of interest in self, that the Christ-life
may increase unto the full freedom of the
social glory of the children of God.

The age of the spirit is come. We are moving into a new cycle of human growth. Close
upon us is the social inspiration of the world,
revealing the home of God in the people, and
the society of the people in God. We cannot
calculate the social development, or deduce the
unseen from the seen. We dare not limit the
power of the spirit to socialize; or put boun-

daries to the social development that may be accomplished by the forces now at work; or survey with our rude instruments and blurred sight the social way in which God may compel our steps. We see not yet how or what God may do, and the Judge of our civilization will do right beyond our unbelieving thought. But we should be getting ready for the social baptism of the Holy Spirit and fire. For the coming revelation of God will be our judgment in the righteousness of Christ, and the communion of our purified humanity in the Holy Ghost. Then the sons and daughters of God will change the glowing dreams of the prophets into enduring social facts.

VI.

THE APPEAL OF REDEMPTION TO PROGRESS.

Rom. vi. 1, 2.

If I supposed it to be very near, I should still try to put off the Golden Age, at least till I had reasoned my reader out of his fears of it; for there is nothing that seems to alarm people so much as the notion of a Golden Age to come. Nothing is really so offensive to the average good man or woman as the notion of human brotherhood. But I think this is not from any innate hatred of one's kind, or a natural disposition to obey the law and the prophets rather than the new commandment they hang upon; for I am a great friend of human nature, and I like it all the better because it has had to suffer so much unjust reproach. It seems to me that we are always mistaking our conditions for our natures, and saying that human nature is greedy and mean and false and cruel, when only its conditions are so. We say you must change human nature if you wish to have human brotherhood; but we really mean that you must change human conditions, and this is quite feasible. It has always been better than its conditions, and ready for new and fitter conditions, although many sages have tried to rivet the old ones upon it, out of some such mistaken kindness as would forbid the crustacean a change of shell. The state of the crustacean after this change takes place is perilous, but with all its dangers it is not so perilous as the effort to keep its old shell on forever would be. — *W. S. Howells*, in " Equality as the Basis of Good Society."

THE question is not whether monoply is to continue. The sun sets every night on a greater majority against it. We are face to face with the practical issue: Is it to go through ruin or reform? Can we forestall ruin by reform? If we wait to be forced by events we shall be astounded to find how much more radical they are than our utopias. Louis XVI. waited until 1793, and gave his head and all his investitures to the people who in 1789 asked only to sit at his feet and speak their mind. Unless we reform of our own free will, nature will reform us by force, as nature does. Our evil courses have already gone too far in producing misery, plagues, hatreds, national enervation. Already the leader is unable to lead, and has begun to drive with judges armed with bayonets and Gatling guns. History is the serial obituary of the men who thought they could drive men. — *Henry D. Lloyd*, in " Wealth Against Commonwealth."

VI.

THE APPEAL OF REDEMPTION TO PROGRESS.

Shall we continue in sin that grace may abound? God forbid. — ROM. vi. 1, 2.

THE community of Christians at Rome seems to have been troubled with the old problem, still so new, of evil and moral redemption. To define the right in distinction from the wrong, and to procure the personal and national practice of the right, the Jew had been trained in an ideal system of law, in some respects the most effective and just the world yet knows; but he had sinned against the law, even to such a degree as to largely destroy the moral value of the law itself. The Greek, like other peoples of the world, had been without the Jew's law and knowledge of right; but he, refusing to walk in the clear moral light of nature, had gayly sinned against

199

his own conscience, faithless to the right he truly knew. There was no difference between Jew and Greek as to moral guilt and need of redemption; no difference, when the light of each was taken into account, as to the depth of failure and the greatness of moral need. All had sinned and come short of that righteousness which is the glory of God in human life.

This raised the question of moral responsibility. How was he who knew he law, interpretative of God and right, better conditioned than he who knew not? The roots of individual redemption reached so deep into the past and far into the future, with moral progress so involved in divine processes which the individual had nothing to do with save accept them, that men were in danger of thinking sin a mere process of virtue, and of losing the sense of individual responsibility in the sense of human universality. In any case, it was clear that a man could not separate himself from the human organism, or consider his individuality as a thing in itself, independent

of the world processes; he could treat himself only as a part and function of the great
whole. And the comprehension of this raised
individual responsibility to the other extreme,
seeming to increase it to the very responsibility of God, but with the same practical
results that its loss produced; when measured
by its responsibility, individual effort was
stricken with the sense of its insignificance.

The question was enlarged beyond measure
by the fact that the death of Jesus, with all
its meanings and issues, was taken to be the
highest expression of the love and thought of
God for man. To the end of the redemptive
economy, the cross would be at once the final
interpreter of God and of the law of human
life; it was henceforth to be the symbol of
progress and moral triumph. Sin had raised
this cross, and nailed upon it the sacred
victim. If sin had thus been, to Hebrew
and other nations alike, the channel of
God's richest grace, the medium of deliverance and moral freedom, why should man be
condemned? If through sin had come man's

greatest good, why not continue in sin that grace might abound?

In answer to the questions raised, the Roman letter is Paul's interpretation of history from the redemptive point of retrospect and prospect. It both anticipates and far transcends the historical philosophy of Hegel. Only incidentally theological, and that with no thought of a dogmatic system, it presents history as a continuous development toward human perfectness. With a mind as masterful as his heart was loving, with an affection as pure as his faith was strong, with a universal seizing hold of the meanings of things, the apostle's vision swept the whole range of human processes, and saw them all to be working out the perfected life. The moral stature and freedom of Jesus was the divine account and perfect work of these processes, the judgment upon them that would never change. With lower than this destiny, the eternal word that dwelt and spoke in all flesh would let no man be satisfied. Towards its attainment all man's undying instincts were driving him, and all his divine impulses bearing him on. Even long after holy passions seemed to have died out of his fallen nature, the sin of man would be punishing him to renewed effort.

With that sacred over-earnestness of his, so burning as to sometimes consume the ties that bound him to his brethren, Paul urged that sin had been working for right, in spite of itself. He saw its seeming triumphs initiating the great movements of moral victory, and its bitter wages buying moral ransom from its hard service. No kind of disaster or disgrace had escaped bearing man nearer to the kingdom of redemption, in whose economy of grace he was henceforth to believe and achieve. Without regard to its seeming makers, history of the worst sort had been helping man to his holy destiny. Pharoah as well as Moses, traders of Sodom as well as Abraham, Esau as well as Jacob, Greek as well as Jew, Pharisee as well as prophet, had been realizing God's great human thought. Whether sin had been necessity or loss, the sense of its guilt held the roots of the idea of redemption, and had made ground for that vision of God in Calvary which makes and exhausts new languages only to widen its meaning with the ages.

But that progress had risen through moral failure was no sign that men could ever choose this method without the certainty of moral death to themselves, whatever God might buy with sin's wages. God forbid that any should continue in sin that grace might abound, for to continue in sin was just the way to impoverish grace. Man being now redeemed, sin was left without excuse. The sacrifice of Christ had brought it into the open, where it could be seen at its strongest, in fatal contrast with the cross ; its strength a delusion, its triumph a defeat, and its reality a fiction. The sacrifice was also the definition of righteousness, so that there need be no more confusion as to its nature and value, no mistake as to its law of service and the reality of its power. This full disclosure of the nature of sin, together with the nature of righteousness, had finished the economy of sin, and initiated the economy of redemption. The redemptive initiative was not a letting-down, but a closing-up, of moral responsibility ; it spread before men a boundless prospect of moral opportunity and adventure, with yet untrod continents of religious resource to be subdued to human uses. Men were no more in bondage to sin, and it had no more dominion over them. They were no longer citizens of the old economy, and were to reckon with righteousness henceforth, and with sin no more. The method and power of sin were forever broken ; and they were to deny it any right to be taken into account, much less regard it as necessary or powerful. The old order of things worked out and ended, and the new begun, they were to quit having faith in sin as a real force, and begin to put their whole faith in righteousness; they were to take to trusting the light that was in them, and cease believing in the darkness. The heart of the whole matter of evil lay in believing in it, in feeling helpless about it and making terms with it, in having more faith in its strength and reality than in the strength and reality of the good. By every sort of analysis and emphasis, Paul tried to make clear that religious safety and growth, moral prosperity and progress, depended not upon believing in wrong, but upon believing in right. Whatever the origin and mystery of sin, it was time to abolish it; and the death on the cross was the abolition act.

Now, I have no thought of using Paul to deny the fact of sin, nor the tragedy of it, in human development. There is little need of that, in these anxious days, with the hand of God heavy on the social conscience, and the question of what to do to be saved become a world interrogation. Never was the sense of sin so deep and universal, the knowledge of wrong so vivid and intense, the feeling of expiation so common — oppressive to some, exhilarating to others. The world's wretchedness seems about to become morally conscious of itself, and to make a stern and holy demand, which must be heard before long, that it be delivered from the body of its death. There are an increasing number to whom life is tolerable only on condition that it may be wholly contributed toward realizing in the common life that perfect good which is the fruit of right relations. "Into a world sadly out of tune," are these being born, as Mrs. Oliphant says of St. Francis, "to be a sign and wonder in the midst of all its self-seekings, its fightings, its traffickings, its dominion of the strong, and oppression of the poor."

The last few years have wrought a swift and significant change in both scientific and popular attitudes toward the problem of evil and redemption. The story of Eden is no longer the joke it was taken to be, a little while ago, when evolutionary thought was young and exuberant, and many scientific discoveries were at hand. Adam and Eve never stood for so much moral meaning as now. The matchless narrative of the fall of man has been robbed of its sad beauty by the literalness of theologians and the stupid accuracy of scientists. It has been divested of its solemnity by religious clownishness. Yet the story is not now hard to understand. Nor does it impress us as being funny. Its divine simplicity is the profoundest explanation of history possible to the inspired imagination. It carries with it an infinite sadness, which only deepens as the course of man lengthens. The ages form no mist that can obscure its idea. It is the story of every human career that finds its way, through the wilderness of trial, from the Eden of innocence to the Calvary of moral freedom. It tells the experience of every man who has lived long enough in the flesh to learn the right and wrong of things.

Nor would I deny that sin has been a method by which the highest good has come. How could it be else, if good came at all, with no other than sinful men through which to realize itself? No doubt Adam's fall was the beginning of wisdom and virtue; that is, when man first awoke to moral consciousness, to the idea of a right in distinction from a wrong, then of course moral struggle and development began. This struggle has been the pro-

gressive realization of God's human thought.
God has not at any time been outwitted by
some stronger force. History is not a joy-
less defeat. God is making the wrong carry
along the right, and is binding man to the
throne of life by bonds of death. The quick
centuries and sad histories, with God and
his universe of life, are toiling in man's behalf, increasing the promise of moral perfection. Behind and within the failure and
shame, the tragedy and violent effort, and
through all the sin of the world, works the
passion of God's love, with the eternal wisdom of it, bringing to hope the strifeless
progress, the holy society; bringing to faith
the law disclosed on Calvary as the final social government. Within the disorders and
perplexities, seeing eyes are discerning the
not yet manifested unity, and hearing ears
are catching the muffled harmony.

But it does not follow that sin has been
a necessity to the development of righteousness. The moral nerve of society has been
fearfully enervated by a vague philosophy,

pervading modern literature even unto the poetry of Browning, and somewhat inhering in evolutionary science, that sin is simply good in the making. While it is true that to the man who chooses the good and refuses the evil, sin becomes the very builder of his virtue, in no sense is sin good, or are we better for having sinned. That God has made it work redemptive good, does not change the fact that redemption brings no gift that might not have been a sinless gain. It was no more necessary for Adam than it was for Jesus to sin; his character might have been proved as the character of Jesus was proved. Sin is not good in the making; it can be nothing else, and nothing else ought it to be, than endless loss. Whatever we may think of it, sin is no constituent or elemental part of life, and was no necessity of moral creation. Sin does not lie in the nature of things human.

Nor does it follow that the showing forth of God in Christ was dependent on sin, or that it would not have come in the due un-

folding of God's thought for man. God did
not act as other than himself in redeeming
man ; he did not act exceptionally in the
sacrifice of the cross. The cross did not
reveal something God was circumstantially
compelled to be or do, in order to repair a
failure. God as truly sacrifices in creation
as in redemption, for sacrifice is the law
of creation. That sacrifice is the law of
God's being and universe, is the meaning of
the saying which we translate as the Lamb
slain before the foundation of the world. It
is because we found our ideas of sacrifice on
sin instead of on righteousness that we get
into pagan confusions about God and man,
and form such rude and immoral doctrines of
their relations. Sacrifice is not dependent
upon sin, but upon the righteousness of love;
sin is not its cause, but its hinderance and
suffering. It was not the sufferings and
death of Jesus that constituted his sacrifice,
but the fruitful offering of his life, which
sin and death antagonized. The substantial
revelation of the cross was not made be-

cause, but in spite of sin; sin did not bring, but long delayed, its coming.

Sin is not something, but the want of something, being nothing in itself. It is willing incompleteness, the negativing of growth, and hence the suicide of life; it becomes guilt, so that we speak of it as a positive and concrete thing, when one refuses to will the right. Sin is a falling back from moral destiny, a failure to endure the holy, selfless struggle of service, which is the cost of being. God himself would cease to be, were he to cease to become, to serve, and give himself. Our first parents ate of the fruit of moral ease; they ceased to become, and their life fell, as our life falls, by the denial of life, instead of the denial of self; and their fall, like ours, was the great fall from the pursuit of right into the pursuit of happiness, from whence come the miseries of the ages, with every sort of tyranny and slavery. The sinfulness of sin is moral abiding in what one is, or in what society is. Continuance in an old organization of life, after a better has been revealed, is what makes sin sinful.

We can thus see why Paul was so terrified at the bare possibility of the delusion that grace might abound through continuance in sin. Grace abounds to the degree that we are sin's enemy, and no more. The struggle against sin is itself the grace of God shining and working in our life. The disaster and guilt of sin are not in discovering that one has sinned, but in staying in sin through the dark imagination that it will overcome itself. The evil heart of unbelief that enters not in and fulfils the divine promises is the one that shamelessly waits for divine chance to add future moral glory to present moral sloth and cowardice. It is content with the historic gain and moral wealth inherited from the past, with the ethical principles and social practices through which the past reached the present, that sets redemption at naught, and changes the grace of God into the moral disgrace of man.

Persistence in progress, with its unceasing change of effort and growth, is therefore the law and revelation of the Christian redemption. What was good yesterday, or good in its method and application, may be so evil when applied to to-day, that to continue in it is death. "It is only a formal rectitude," says Hegel, "deserted by the living Spirit and by God, which those who stand upon ancient right and order maintain." The sum of human duty is the moral obligation of the man, or the society, immediately to abandon a present organization of life the moment a possible better is conceived or discovered. And the better is always at hand. Perpetual transition, growth that rests only in increase, is the only rational state of society, the only moral condition for man. Religion is continuous progress, through the moral adventure of faith in the ideal; while sin is the denial of the best possibility one sees or knows, in favor of the worth and reality of the good one is or has. A progress that shall move on, to use a phrase of Goethe's, "without haste, but without rest, like the stars in heaven," is the ideal of social faith. When our ancestors quit their pestilent and unbelieving habit of trying to govern us, and are great enough to contribute their faith to the future without imposing their will upon it, trusting God enough to set their children free in his hands, then progress will move on by fulfilment, and destruction will be among the old things passed away. When a race of men is born that shall accept unceasing change and growth as the law of blessedness, and be reconciled to perpetual transition as the only living condition, then the economy of redemption will have finished its work, and the kingdom of heaven will be fully come, with human life lived in the vision of God.

The continuous human rise from subjection into freedom may be justly claimed as a revelation of science, by which the process or idea is called evolution. The term redemption is not an altogether happy one, when the arbitrary meanings attached to it are considered. But the term evolution is no more satisfactory, when we take into account all the moral facts and forces of progress. So, until science and theology are each sufficiently delivered from the wisdom of their own conceits to hear each other's testimony, with a decent sense of having something to learn from each other, and are socialized enough to co-operate for the discovery of the one law and human meaning of development, we in religious spheres of effort had better stick to the old term of redemption. And, though I am no friend to dogmatic theology of any sort, I must here confess that, so far as I can see, theology is fairly ready to hear the conclusions of science, while science regards religious contributions with dogmatic or derisive contempt, when not with indifference or ignorance. But our systems of faith and our systems of science will not always remain apart, nor will they continue to be dogmatic; they will each sometime become a social evangelism, a brother-discipleship in the one human school of God; and all pursuits of knowledge, of whatsoever sort, will at last become one holy apostolate of social faith. In fact, the newer science, though using different terms, is already apostolic with the early

Christian idea of a redeemed and perfected human life, — a life that has subdued the physical forces, to which it has hitherto been subjected, unto obedient and harmonious social services. Without either science or theology meaning it, evolution and redemption are coming to be synonymous terms for one human revelation and destiny, one final strifeless progress.

But that progress will be reached only through the widest and most daring application of the law by which Christ redeems. They who discern on Calvary the disclosure of a deeper, vaster law than the ways of men and nature we call laws, who read the cross as the law of the physical universe as well as of moral redemption, and who proceed to interpret that law in economic and civic terms, will save the world many dark ages, and prepare the way of the holy society.

The failure of Christ's redemptive resources is not in any lack of their quantity or quality, but in the notion that they will work redemption without being applied. The superstition

that righteousness will increase without adventure and sacrifice, that "things will come
out right somehow" without our making them
right, is sin doing its worst. To believe
that grace will abound without effort, or as
its substitute, is the supreme delusion. To
practise an economy of sin, while we live in
an economy of redemption, is the supreme
anarchy. To organize life by a law of selfishness, when we are under the government of
the law of sacrifice, is the supreme foolish-
ness. To go on recognizing evil as a fact to
which we must be reconciled, to treat competition as an economy we must make terms
with, to regard the old self-interest as a law
to which we must submit, to reckon with
moral ignorance as the first thing to be accepted in order to be practical, and all this
in the face of the offered Christ, is the
supreme atheism. Against this atheism the
scientific revelation of love as natural law
will not prevail, nor will the signs of change
with which these anxious days of social strain
are instinct and messianic; only that absolute

judgment that shall not leave one faithless stone upon another will prevail against it for the redeemed progress.

The guilt of this atheism is upon us all, and upon all our ways and works. By faith and practice, individually and collectively, religiously and politically, commercially and educationally, we go on sinning that grace may abound. To the common thought, sin abounds much more than grace ; and therefore the common thought reckons with sin, and makes grace of practically small account. In a profound sense, the most religious of us reckon with sin too much and with righteousness too little. When dealing with life, the most of us believe a great deal more in the devil than we believe in God. As John Ruskin said, we really think the laws of the devil more practicable than the laws of God, however much we deny our belief. We like to think so, for we thus evade the very responsibility the economy of redemption puts upon us. With our lips we confess that the kingdom and the power and the glory are God's ; with our lives we confess that they are

Satan's. We undertake our enterprises, not alone of business or politics, but of religion and reform as well, by making terms with evil ; by reckoning with it as the real power. That terrible temptation typified by Jesus in the wilderness—so forced upon us by the outer view of experience and history — to make concessions to evils honored by established order and ancient custom, in order to obtain a modicum of righteousness, still deceives and overcomes our ideals, as it did not deceive and disarm the one clear-visioned Son of man. Movements for holy national life surrendered to mere diplomacy, the kingdom of heaven hid in ecclesiastical politics and the prayings and preachings of costly temples, wide social impulses lost in compromises which the religious effect between them and the powerful in market and state, expectations of the toiling poor that perish in the philanthropies of rich buyers of legislation, municipal reforms committed to the moneyed respectability that has really looted and debauched the city, are all ways of sinning that grace may abound. These are our modern ways, fervently encouraged by all sorts of teachers, of continuing in injustice and covetousness, that justice and brotherly love may abound. At bottom, they are forms of the unconscious devil worship that rules society as official religion or as business, as the triumph of grace or as political economy, as wise management or as clear thinking, as judicious effort or as common sense. They are all the persistence of the atheism that takes on a religious fright when man would rise above money; that sees civilization exterminated by the doctrine that life is more sacred than property; that zealously denies the faith for to-day in the name of the faith of yesterday.

The present condition of civilization is a universal instance of the anarchy of thought and effort that follows the persistence of the modes and experiences of yesterday over the newer life of to-day. Industrialism rose out of feudalism through conditions of competition. The economist wrote down the observable phenomena of these competitive conditions as natural economic laws, to which be

social dominion and power and glory forever.
A deeper insight might have shown that industrial progress would arise in spite of competition, rather than because of it, through various
forms of modified or unconscious co-operation,
by which competition was qualified or avoided.
Competition will yet be defined, in relation
to human development, as a past mode or
condition, but not a law; and a condition
which human life instinctively finds the
quickest way to escape. A better evolutionary science will one day show us that co-
operation, more than competition, has been
the great law of survival in nature. Even
if it had been as fierce as Mr. Darwin pic-
tured, it did not follow that competition would
keep on when life became human and ethical. Quite the reverse might follow, as some
of the ablest analysts of competition in ńat-
ural development now insist. "A real capacity for change, and that for the better, an
impulse of perfectibility," is that by which
Hegel distinguishes man from "merely natural objects, in which we find always one and

the same stable character." And if competition really were the law of industrial development, it does not at all follow that it should be the law of the social organization of industry.

At its human best, competition is always a moral evil, though under certain imagined conditions it appears to be moral gain and social vigor. It is profane in theory, when judged by the teachings of Jesus, or by the moral reason, and causes the worst instincts of life to triumph. It makes the average life an uncertain struggle for bread, and a degrading game of chance. It brings the people into wretched economic subjection, with political, intellectual, and even religious subjection logically following. It involves the whole human organism in a strife corrupting from height to depth, cursing ideas and practices alike, poisoning every motive, and perverting every action.

But the social fact, more effectively than any social idealism, is denying the right of competition to persist, or to be called law.

Competition is becoming impracticable. It will no longer work; it is not working, save for both human and industrial death, with political and social anarchy. To all but the dogmatic economist, and those industrial fanatics who have caught his trick of defining every thing socially oppressive and monstrous as natural law, it is clear that the competitive system has exhausted its possibilities for progress, that it can only continue for social disaster and disintegration. Unless supplanted by a co-operative civilization, it may bring the universal woe so long foretold. "It is not to be denied," confesses Mr. Herbert Spencer, in his argument against socialism, "that the evils are great, and form a large set-off from the benefits. The system under which we at present live fosters dishonesty and lying. It prompts adulterations of countless kinds; it is answerable for the cheap imitations which eventually in many cases thrust the genuine articles out of the market; it leads to the use of short weights and false measures; it introduces bribery, which vitiates most trading relations, from those of the manufacturer and buyer down to those of the shopkeeper and servant; it encourages deception to such an extent that an assistant who cannot tell a falsehood with a good face is blamed; and often it gives the conscientious trader the choice between adopting the malpractices of his competitors, or greatly injuring his creditors by bankruptcy. Moreover, the extensive frauds, common throughout the commercial world and daily exposed in lawcourts and newspapers, are largely due to the pressure under which competition places the higher industrial classes." [1] And Mr. Spencer calls all these "minor evils," compared to the unjust distribution which the system procures.

It would surely seem that the appeal of the deeper social conscience against our competitive system would be the most welcome and authoritative voice; that the thought of continuing in the system, with any expectation of justice or social morality, would be

[1] "A Plea for Liberty," p. 4.

regarded by good men as irrational and blasphemous. In the light of the present social facts, it is well-nigh as immoral and absurd to talk about honorable competition as it would be to talk about honorable burglary. In the actual human situation in which we stand, our commercial, political, educational, and religious cant about peaceful rivalry, honorable competition, and the like, are as disgusting as the "holy whine" of any emaciated pietism; and we all know we are hypocrites in the use of such phrases. Yet economists, monopolists, and clergymen would have us continue in competition, that social justice and religion, commercial integrity and individual enterprise, may abound; that the poor, who possibly average a few cents more a day than they did some four or five hundred years ago, may prosper and be grateful. And by this stupendous weight of intellectual humbuggery and moral hypocrisy, solemnly posing as clear thinking and judicious effort, we the sons of God suffer social progress to be overborne — till the day of reckon-

ing. But need we wait for reckonings of
fire, for suffering such as the world may
have never known, to teach us obedience to
the better ? As we behold the doctors of
economics and the doctors of religion standing in the midst of the social fact to bless
it, with the high priests of business supporting their right hand and political traffickers
their left, the irony of the situation should
call us to sanity, and show us the imbecility
of our unfaith, before the social woe rises
into universal wrath.

There are terrible perplexities, I know,
breaking the purest hearts. However hard
or devoutly our wills be set against it, so
long as the system exists, we are all competitors in some degree. All of us who live
in any measure of comfort live more or less
by economic stealing, no matter what our
occupation or intentions. Our comforts are
bought with the poverty, and even the lives,
of beaten men and women. It is practically
true, and ought to be true, that none of us
can extricate ourselves from the social dis-

grace and pain until the whole social life is extricated. We cannot sleep, eat, wear clothes, travel, educate ourselves, read books, attend public worship, without participating in the social wrong and bearing the social guilt.

But, withal, we need not continue in the sin of the system under the delusion that grace may thereby abound. There is a divine, as well as a devilish, complicity in evil. We may be in, while we are not of, organized wrong. We may war and sacrifice against the competition that besets us, participating in it only for its overthrow and the social rescue. We may confess our part in the social stealing, and partake of it only to expose it for the social deliverance. We may help the prosperous to understand how the system makes them social thieves, in spite of themselves ; pious maybe, and honorable, but none the less thieves, to be brought to judgment with the system. We may go with them to the repentance of social sacrifice — the sacrifice that will take no more of the prosperity of the world until the kingdom of God be come. If we are in the system as men who will not tolerate it for a moment, nor make peace with it in a single attitude, but who will profit by it as little as possible, while seeking to be to it of the highest redemptive utility, then we are ending the existing order and preparing for the better one. Thus engaging in the social expiation, we may deny in the name of our Christ, by the power of his blood and living presence, by his redemption and kingship, that there is one wrong thing in our own life, or in the life of the world, that needs to continue unremedied for an hour; we may affirm that grace will instantly abound in the smallest honest effort to right the wrong, making that effort a fruit and glory of the new earth.

In that famous Leyden sermon of Pastor Robinson to the departing Pilgrims, reported twenty-six years later by Edward Winslow, in which he spoke his confidence that "the Lord had more truth and light yet to break forth out of his holy word," he exhorted

them to remember that it was "not possible
the Christian world should come so lately
out of such thick anti-Christian darkness, and
that full perfection of knowledge should break
forth at once." "He took occasion also to
bitterly bewail the state and condition of the
Reformed Churches, which were come to a
period in religion, and would go no further
than the instruments of their Reformation,"
Luther and Calvin, "a misery much to be la-
mented. For though they were precious shining lights in their times, yet God hath not
revealed his whole will to them ; and were
they now living, saith he, they would be as
ready and willing to embrace further light as
that they had received." [1] If we, who glorify
by our words the past faith and mighty work
of this Moses of the Pilgrims, would practise
his religious statesmanship, and heed his warning in our relation to present problems, we
would then glorify Robinson and the Pilgrims
in truth, with Jesus and his prophets and
apostles as well, and save to the social move-

[1] "The Pilgrim Fathers of New England," Dr. John Brown, p. 189.

ment the leadership of the religion from which noble leaders are turning bitterly away. Unfaith in the better is the essence of all atheism ; it bears the sad fruits of revolutions that destroy the present and revert to the past, ere able to gain strength for progress and make way for the better than the good that is.

Our habits manifest this atheism because the curse of it is upon all our systems of thought. The long line of fatalistic philosophies, making man the tragic play of dual and jealous forces, still make for fear and bondage, still hold men back from freedom, and the manhood of the sons of God. The Asiatic fatalisms disputed by the great drama of Æschylus, the moral despair of the gnostics, the Augustinian price God paid to Satan for man, the irresponsible sovereignty enthroned by Calvin and at Westminster, the Spencerian unknowable and its unmoral energies, the economic laws set forth by the economists, are all modes of one and the same monstrous delusion that power is other and

stronger than right. The old gnostic dualism
has laboriously and firmly wrought its morbid
scepticism into the theological redemption,
that does not redeem; into the theological
atonement, that presents the greatest conceivable lie as the most saving religious
truth; into the theological righteousness, that
practically confesses the devil to be the world's
real lord. The self-interest and self-love of
the moral sciences are the old sad unfaith in
the all-goodness of the world forces, crystal-
lized and made small by the puerilities of
school culture. The mysterious fates of the
east are the economic laws of the west. The
Oriental faith in evil reincarnates itself in
Augustine, to be restated in Christian terms
and Roman forms; the Augustinian faith is
systematically restated by Calvin; and the
Spencerian philosophy is the Calvinistic theology restated in modern materialistic and scientific terms. These each have at heart the
same desperate and baneful faith in the in-
herent and irreconcilable antagonism between
righteousness and the nature of things. They

are all, in some degree, the persistence of
the ancient fear, with its dualistic faiths and
fatalistic philosophies, that evil holds the human situation, and must be propitiated if life
is to be safely or prosperously lived.

But lift up your eyes, and you may behold
a new world forming in human faith, en-
sphered in a new universe, and a new man
rising from the struggle, the agony, the blood,
the fear, and the dust. Prometheus is unbind-
ing himself. Of the dominion of evil, of
fates, of mysteries, of necessities, of unknowable energies, of economic laws, we are to
have an end; these are the delusion, the lie —
the monsters of the night, ghosts that now
vanish with the dawn. Man is greater than
these, their anointed king, and king because
trustful servant of all. The fates are to be
of man's making, and the forces of nature his
glad servants, the winds and the waves obeying him, while he pursues the highest, free
from fear of the unknown, walking in the
light, with faith to dare and to adventure
in social quest and moral discovery. Man is

rising stronger than the superstition, alike
theological and scientific, alike political and
economic, that power is other than right, and
that only self-interest can summon to the
highest effort. This time, when the temple
of power falls, Samson will stand, and will receive his sight with his freedom. And upon
the ruins of power he will build the temple
of service, which is the temple of the redeemed and glorified humanity, the abiding
temple of God. The word of God is being
made flesh universal, and we are beholding
its glory in the divine resolve with which
man is nerving himself for this social task.
" In these days," so William Morris makes
John Ball say, "are ye building a house which
shall not be overthrown, and the world shall
not be too great or too little to hold it; for
indeed it shall be the world itself, set free
from evil-doers for friends to dwell in."
" Therefore," he concludes, "there is nought
that can undo us except our own selves and
our hearkening to soft words from those who
would slay us." So he cries to men " to do

great deeds or to repent them that they were ever born." [1]

O brothers, why dwell we in ancient fears of the dark, when the glory of the breaking light is waking to service and freedom? We are not helpless, nor in bondage; nor is there anything to fear, save the fear that would keep us from having faith and being free. It is always infinitely easier, if we only knew it, to realize the highest conceivable right than the relative or moderate right. The kingdom and the power and the glory are God's, and not the devil's. Evil is not a power and a reality, and has no right to be reckoned with, or to exact terms, or to receive tribute. God forbid that we should continue to be led into lies by the delusion that grace will abound in our sin. The world is redeemed, with sin no more in dominion over us, and the exhilaration and prophecy of a strifeless progress in the air. "It is time," cries a noble voice of the hour, "for men to escape from yesterday, and to govern to-day by to-morrow and the day after."

[1] "A Dream of John Ball."

Prophecy is not mockery, but reason at its highest. The vision of the new earth, the righteous society, is the history of what is becoming; no other assumption as the basis of thought and action is good sense. It is irrational to conceive of selfishness and strife as a permanent mode of activity. " In the creation of a just God," says Charles Wagner, "evil cannot be more than a transitory state, the result of error and ignorance," to disappear through "the efforts of men who live outside of themselves." The dream of moral wholeness, of a social life that is a holy communion and not a struggle and strife, is not a noble illusion. The long tragedy of effort will have its human perfectness at last. The creation shall be delivered from its bondage of corruption into the liberty of the glory of the sons of God.

The seeds of human sacrifice will then grow into trees of life, and put forth their leaves for the healing of the nations. This winter of doubt and sorrow, this night of fear, these clouded and sometimes starless skies, this baffling of effort, this sickness of hope, will then have gone. The social springtime will awake, never to sleep; and the summer of God will come, and not fail with ripening life. The flowers of love will bloom in the warmth of a passion as pure as the breath of angels; in a human life whose every impulse is social ecstasy, and every act a sacrament of service. And in the fulness of time, men will eat no more of the tree of the knowledge of good and evil, having entered the joy of the life that knows neither merit nor demerit. Then our human life will endlessly rise in a strife-less progress, and become the perfect music of God's great human thought.